What's the Difference?

Books by Norman Moss

WHAT'S THE DIFFERENCE?—A BRITISH/AMERICAN DICTIONARY
MEN WHO PLAY GOD: THE STORY OF THE H-BOMB

What's the Difference?

A British / American Dictionary

NORMAN MOSS

HARPER & ROW, PUBLISHERS

NEW YORK, EVANSTON, SAN FRANCISCO, LONDON

FIRST EDITION

Designed by C. Linda Dingler

Library of Congress Cataloging in Publication Data

Moss, Norman.
    What's the difference?
    1. English language—Dictionaries. 2. Americanisms—Dictionaries. 3. English language in Great Britain—Dictionaries. I. Title.
PE2835.M6   428′.1   72-9140
ISBN 0-06-013096-2

Contents

Introduction

This book is intended primarily to help Britons and Americans understand and communicate better with one another. The need for such a book occurred to me often as I watched some Anglo-American misunderstanding caused by words having different meanings. Like the time I heard an American student at Cambridge University telling some English friends how he climbed over a locked gate to get into his college and tore his pants, and one of the Englishmen asked in confusion, "But how could you tear your pants without tearing your trousers?"

This book lists those words that are different in the two languages in their common usage. The criterion is whether a word is familiar to most people in one country or the other, not whether it is listed in a dictionary. There are words listed in Webster's *Third New International Dictionary* that are in current use in England but that most Americans never hear and would not understand, and some in the *Oxford English Dictionary* that have not been heard in conversation in Britain for a century. And Webster's is not much help to an Englishman who finds himself perplexed by, for instance, some of the baroque Americanisms of *Portnoy's Complaint*.

Some words in one language are unknown in the other, e.g., Britain's *Bath-chair*, *loo*, and *panda car*, and America's *highball* and *raunchy*. Others have different meanings that can cause misunderstandings, like *fag*, *knock up*, and *tights*. A few even have the exact opposite meaning in the two languages, like *enjoin, public school,* and *table* (as a verb). A few others are close enough to be understood, but are included here for the benefit of those who want to be able to speak and write the other language as the natives do.

Where it is appropriate, I have tried to give an indication of the verbal or social context in which a word is likely to be used, as well as a definition. Most Americans know roughly what the word *bloody* means, but not what kind of place they may be thrown out of for using it.

Since the criterion for inclusion is what is commonly heard, this leaves much room for disagreement. Heard by whom? Language varies by age, occupation, social level, and geography. In the case of many words, the linguistic dividing line is not the Atlantic but age; young people on both sides of the Atlantic use terms in common which are alien to their parents. Most of the language of the youth-drugs-underground culture is as international as its attitudes. The division, on campuses, of people into "straights" and "heads" began in Britain almost at the same time that it did in the United States.

A word that is foreign to one person will not be foreign to another. New Yorkers and Washingtonians hear more words from Britain than Midwesterners. Americans who go to the theater and to foreign movies regularly are likely to use more British-English words than others who do not. Some people inherit words from Britain through their families. In Britain, young people use more American words than their elders, Londoners more than others. Any reader may find words listed here as belonging to the other language that are familiar to him. The chances are that they are not familiar to some of his fellow countrymen.

Considerations of what words do and do not belong in both languages are complicated by the speed with which the two languages are changing, both within themselves and in relation to each other. Words go out of use and others arise within a decade. *Soul, frag* (American), *gazump,* and *U.D.I.* (British) were unknown a few years ago but will certainly be around for a long time.

The two languages are moving closer together; the accents, speech rhythms, and words of each country are becoming more familiar to the other. Increased travel across the Atlantic is one factor. There are others which both result from this process and assist it further: the acceptance of David Frost as a major television personality in America and not an exotic visitor, impossible fifteen years ago; and the acceptance of leading commentators with North American voices on British television, not only on the national networks but on a regional service like Tyne-Tees, which at this writing employs a delectable North American girl as a reporter/news reader; the wide circulation in Britain of American magazines; and the practice of American publishers of reprinting books from British publishers' plates, and vice versa. Currently, television's "Sesame Street" is creating a generation of preschool children in Britain who talk to their parents about the "closet" and the "trash can," and finish their alphabet "x, y, zee."

The movement of words is mostly eastward. Every year, more and more words that were exclusively American are found also in the spoken and written language of Britain. A generation ago, the use in Britain of the word *guy,* or *campus,* would stamp one unmistakably as an American or a Canadian. Today these words fall from the most purely British lips.

This process has been going on for a long time. Almost as soon as the British colonies were established in North America, words and expressions came back and were infiltrated into the language of the mother country. Some of them originated with neighboring settlers in North America who spoke other European languages, some came from American Indian languages; these are still the principal source of exclusively American words to this day. Words such as *bluff* (meaning a feature of the landscape), *canoe,* and *squatter* arrived from America in the eighteenth century, a little while after the potato and the turkey. H. L. Mencken, in *The American Language,* lists American phrases that were used by such quintessentially English writers of the Victorian period as Dickens and Thackeray, almost certainly in ignorance of their origin. It is indeed surprising how quickly immigrant words become integrated, their recent arrival and place of origin forgotten. How many Britons today using the words *doodle, fan,* and *grapevine* realize that they came from America in the 1930s and were almost unknown in Britain before then? Some other words in common use, such as *flashpoint, gimmick,* and *phoney,* are more recent imports still.

Usually, the importation of American words into Britain has encountered a linguistic snobbery that is only one part of the cultural snobbery that bedeviled Anglo-American relations for such a long time. In the eighteenth century, Samuel Johnson, as lexicographer, dismissed "the American dialect" as a corruption of English. Frederick Marryat, the author of *Mr. Midshipman Easy,* who followed the custom of many Victorian authors in visiting America and publishing a diary of his travels, wrote: "It is remarkable how debased the language has become after a short period in America." In 1930, Sir Alfred Knox, a Conservative Member of Parliament, called in the House of Commons for a limit on the importation of American films, explaining: "The words and accent are perfectly disgusting, and there can be no doubt that such films are an evil influence on our language." And speaking of films, it was only a few years ago that, when Marlon Brando played Napoleon in a film, some English critics remarked loftily on the risibility of hearing Napoleon speak American phrases in an American accent. It was left to a letter writer to *The Times* to point out that for Napoleon to use British phrases in a British accent would have been no less anomalous, since he actually spoke French.

For that matter I myself, some years ago, worked on a British newspaper published in Paris under a liverish chief subeditor (he would be chief copy editor on an American paper) who was incensed by the fact that several of his subeditors were American, so that examples of the American language were constantly getting into the copy thrust under his nose. He used to insist that American English was quite simply broken English, as spoken by central European peasants who had just disembarked on the pier at Hoboken (or sometimes, in this exegesis, coolies newly disembarked at San Francisco).

Mark Twain responded to British pretension to linguistic superiority in the cocky tone of the successful upstart. "The King's English is not the King's. It's a joint stock company, and Americans own most of the shares," he wrote, in Pudd'nhead Wilson's journal. A few other American writers since then have felt the need to emphasize the separateness of the American language, as well as of American literature.

Today there is no such pattern of attack and justification. There is, in Britain, little pretension to linguistic superiority, and a wide acceptance on both sides that the language is a shared property and heritage. Britain is neither chauvinistic nor culturally isolationist. The age of the common man favors the American language (culturally, as opposed to politically, the Left in Britain has always been pro-American). In fact, it is now chic to use American terms, in a way that, in another age, it was chic to use French terms, so that they appear often in voguishly sophisticated publications. In recent weeks in Britain, as I write, a women's page columnist in *The Observer* has written about a man "laying his wife," a *Sunday Times* column referred to a "New York hooker," and the *New Statesman* headed a book review simply "Chutzpah."

Generalizations about the two languages are as risky and prone to exceptions as are generalizations about the two peoples, but I'll risk a few observations.

British speech tends to be less general and directed more, in its nuances of meaning, at a subgroup of the population. This can become a kind of code, in which few words are spoken because each, along with its attendant murmurings and pauses, carries a wealth of meaning that rests on shared assumptions and attitudes. No pauses are more pregnant than these British pauses. When a Cockney reacts to a situation with a loaded "Aye-aye . . . ." or a girl from an upper-crust family with "After all, it's a bit much, isn't it?" the speaker is assuming that the listener's background and reactions are so similar to his own that he will be comprehended instantly, and will not be asked, for instance, "Much what?" In periods of Conservative Party government, when the governing group is drawn from a narrower social background than it is in a Labour Party government, men considered for high office have been rejected on private advice such as—in its entirety —"He's a bit hot . . . y'know?" (The traditional Englishman's reputation for taciturnity stems from his tendency to remain within his own social group, where there isn't much to say because everybody knows the same things and feels the same way about them.)

In America, unlike in Britain, there is really such a thing as "journalese." That is, there are words that are used only in journalism, that are seen in newsprint and heard in newscasts and nowhere else, words like *gridiron, leatherneck,* and *parley.*

The American language has less regard than the English for grammatical form and will bulldoze its way across distinctions rather than steer a path between them. It will casually use one form of word for another, turning nouns into verbs, as with *audition, author, fund,* and *host,* and vice versa. This practice also is starting to spread to Britain. Since the civil strife began in Northern Ireland, even the serious British newspapers have used the noun *shoot-out* and the verb *gun down.*

However, this bluntness is not seen in the heart of language, the relation of words to meaning. American speech is not more direct and forthright than British. If anything, it tends to flabbiness, loading sentences with circumlocutions and abstractions, and inflating some words so that they lose strength and substance, words like *great* and *disaster.* A Briton can be misled by this, thinking if an American responds to a suggestion with "Terrific!" that this signifies rapturous enthusiasm, whereas it is only a polite assent.

In this connection, it is interesting to note that when, some years ago, Professor Alan Ross, the British linguist, published a celebrated study of upper-class and non-upper-class language in Britain, classifying words and phrases as U (for upper-class) and non-U, most Americans writing about it missed the point entirely. They assumed that it was the upper crust who would use the genteel, pussyfooting term, whereas in almost every instance it was the non-U term that was more genteel and circumlocutory, the U the more direct—a product of the U person's natural confidence.

I remember when I was a reporter in the London bureau of the Associated Press, coming back one time to the office with a story about an important sale of paintings, in which I quoted a baronet as saying that somebody had "plonked down a hundred thousand smackers." The news editor was one of those Americans who see and portray England as a place where doddering dukes grope their way through pea-soup fogs dratting the fact that they've dropped their blasted monocles. He wouldn't allow the phrase in the story because he said Americans would not recognize an English baronet who talked like that. I wasted a good deal of time trying to persuade him not only that this was what the man had said, but that this was just the sort of thing he *would* say.

Yet, sometimes, it is the American language that is the more muscular of the two, for instance, in the hands of some of the finest American prose stylists, like Hemingway, Fitzgerald, and Salinger. In different ways, either British or American may be more robust, elegant, precise, or colorful.

The title of this dictionary deserves a note of explanation. Some Britons may object that there is no such thing as the "British language," that Britons speak English. It is true that this is the language which, along with its users, conquered Welsh and the Gaelic of Scotland and Ireland, and that it is certainly not in its origins a Scottish or a Welsh language. But to call this an "English/American Dictionary" would imply that Americans do not speak English. So the word *British* is used here to refer to the predominant languge spoken in the British Isles, as distinct from that spoken in other parts of the English-speaking world.

A few words more about what is and is not to be found here. Meanings that are common to the two laguages are not necessarily included, even where the word is included with another meaning. For instance, in the British/American section, the word *chemist* is defined as a druggist. It is not explained that this word in Britain also means a scientist whose field is chemistry, since it means this in America also. Occasionally, the common meaning is included with an explanation where it might cause confusion otherwise. The sole criterion is what is useful.

Sporting terms are not included except where they are used outside the context of the game. If an American goes to a cricket match, he expects to hear unfamiliar words that he would not hear anywhere else. However, he may be talking to an Englishman about anything and hear that someone is "on a sticky wicket." Just as, if the Englishman has fallen among Americans, he might hear it said that someone has "two strikes against him." So the cricket term *wicket* is defined, and the baseball term *strike*. In other areas, specialized terms are included and explained if the nonspecialist may encounter them, shopping for the household, in business, or in a newspaper—in the classified advertisements or in the political or financial columns, for instance.

One other class of words deserves mention, though not inclusion in a dictionary. There are some words that are in the languages of both countries, but that seem to come with the accent of only one. For instance, an American would be unlikely to use the word *bottom,* as in "He fell on his bottom," or *crafty,* as in "He's a crafty lad," though he would understand these words instantly. Similarly, there are words which, though perfectly acceptable in Britain, sound more natural on American lips, like *liquor* and *vacation.*

Words are not included here that are particular to only one part of the country (an exception is made with some Cockney words, which are heard outside the boundaries of London and in any case are more likely than other regional terms to be encountered by Americans). There are Yiddish words used by both Jews and Gentiles in New York that are unknown in the rest of America, and Spanish words heard only in California, while the rural South has a whole vocabulary of its own. There is no attempt to include here archaic words, however colorful or philologically interesting. Differences in spelling are not included, what the pseudonymous American poet Firth, in his poem *Orthography*, calls "The lure of the East when Kipling spells 'pyjamas.' "

I have tried to make this dictionary comprehensive, but not exhaustive.

British / American

AA category, *n.* a movie in this category is passed by the Board of Film Censors for showing with the proviso that no one under 14 may be admitted.

A category, *n.* a movie rating equivalent to an R; the film has been passed by the Board of Film Censors with a warning to parents that they may find it unsuitable for children. The A stands for Adult. Other ratings are AA, U, and X (this last the same as in America).

accumulator, *n.* 1. a storage battery, as in a car. 2. in racing, a combination of bets in which the winnings on one race, if any, are added to the stake in the next one.

advert, *n.* short for advertisement. The American equivalent is "ad."

afters, *n.* dessert. Used mostly by or to children.

aggro, *n.* (colloq.) rough stuff, fighting. A newish term; street gang language. It comes from "aggravation."

aircraftsman, *n.* an R.A.F. rank equivalent to airman.

airing cupboard, *n.* a closet built around a hot-water pipe or tank, so that newly-dried clothes can be warmed there.

air marshal, *n.* an R.A.F. rank equivalent to general. There are also air vice marshals below and air chief marshals above.

airscrew, *n.* propeller. This is the term used within the aviation industry; outside it, people say "propeller."

airship, *n.* dirigible.

alderman, *n.* in Britain, a senior member of a borough or town council, chosen from among and by the councillors. Aldermen do not form a separate body. The office is extinct from May, 1974.

A-levels, *n.* an important exam taken at college-entrance level, in three subjects.

Alf Garnett, *prop. n.* British television's equivalent of Archie Bunker, or a person holding those views. Actually, since Alf Garnett came first, it would be truer to say that Archie Bunker is America's Alf Garnett.

all, *comb. adj.* (colloq.) used following certain other words, it means emphatically, "absolutely nothing," as in the common phrases **damn-all, bugger-all,** and **sod-all.** The last two are vulgar. The mythical Welsh village in which Dylan Thomas set his poetic play *Under Milk Wood* is called Llareggub (many Welsh names begin with a double *l*). This was a joke on the British Broadcasting Corporation, which first commissioned it, the name being "bugger-all" spelled backward.

allotment, *n.* a small plot rented out for growing vegetables or flowers. In industrial towns, many people grow vegetables on allotments.

almoner, *n.* a social worker in a hospital.

Alsatian, *n.* German shepherd dog.

Anglo-Indian, *prop. adj.* of a British family long resident in India. When India was part of the British Empire, this referred to a whole class of people and way of life.

anorak, *n.* parka.

Antipodes, *prop. n.* Australia and New Zealand.

approved school, *n.* a reform school for boys or girls up to the age of 16.

après-ski, *adj.* refers to clothes for wearing on a skiing holiday when off the ski slopes.

apropos, *adj.* relevant. It can be used to begin a sentence as a substitute for "Talking about . . ." as in "Apropos my Aunt Matilda . . ."

argy-bargy, *n.* (colloq.) empty talk.

arse, *n.* ass, in the anatomical sense; fanny. **arse over tit** (colloq.) head over heels in a fall (or as, allegedly, more educated people might say, "base over apex").

articled, *adj.* appointed a lawyer-in-training in a legal office.

articulated, *adj.* made up of several different parts. An **articulated lorry** is a trailer truck.

artiste, *n.* a stage performer. Used for a member of a ballet troupe and, apart from that, mostly for people on the outer fringes of the theatrical profession, as a pretentious term. Vaudeville performers and strippers are often called "artistes," but not actors or actresses on the London stage.

aspidistra, *n.* a plant with large leaves often grown in pots. Because a certain class of shabby-genteel home often used to have an aspidistra in the parlor window, it is sometimes taken as a symbol of that class's social attitudes, either proudly or derisively, as in Gracie Fields' song "The Biggest Aspidistra in the World" and George Orwell's novel *Keep the Aspidistra Flying.*

ass, *n.* fool. The term is much less rude than it is in American, because it does not mean a part of the anatomy but a donkey. The other is **arse** (see above). It implies foolish behavior in public, acting like a buffoon, rather than simple lack of intelligence. "Major Yammerton was rather a peculiar man, inasmuch as he was an ass without being a fool." From *Ask Mama* by Robert Surtees, published in 1859.

assessor, *n.* a claims adjuster in insurance.

athletics team, *n.* track team.

aubergine, *n.* eggplant.

au pair, *n.* a foreign girl who stays with a family and helps with the housework and children, in exchange for room and board and a small salary. She is usually learning English and is often of the same social class as the family with which she is staying.

aye-aye, *interj.* a phrase that means "There's more to this than meets the eye," and points to some further, usually murky, significance. It could be a rejoinder to "He seems to have a lot of money all of a sudden," or

"I bought something interesting in Copenhagen."

back benches, *n.* the benches in the House of Commons where the rank-and-file members sit. Members of the government and the shadow cabinet sit across the floor from each other on the front benches. A **back bencher** is a rank-and-file Member of Parliament.

back-hander, *n.* (colloq.) payment on the side, usually illicit.

back-log, *n.* this stands for the same thing as in American but always carries a negative connotation. In Britain it means a pileup of something that cannot easily be cleared and has implications of a logjam. A businessman might say woefully, "I've got a back-log of work," as an apology for late delivery.

bag, *n.* the amount of game killed or caught in a day.

bag, *v.* to catch or kill, usually in hunting. In schoolboy language, to claim something.

bags, *n.* (colloq.) 1. lots. There is no singular use in this sense. 2. trousers. Rather old-fashioned. 3. Staking a claim, in schoolboy language. "Bags I go!" means "I want to go and I said it first."

bailiff, *n.* as well as a court official, this also means the manager of an estate or farm.

bairn, *n.* infant. Mostly Scottish and North country.

bakshee, *n.* (colloq.) something for nothing. From the Arab beggar's plea for "baksheesh," brought back by the army from the Middle East. Often pronounced and occasionally spelled "bukshee."

balaclava, *n.* a warm woolen headgear that covers the ears. First worn by soldiers at Balaclava during the Crimean War.

balls-up, *n.* (colloq.) snafu, a fouled-up situation.

Banbury cake, *n.* a kind of mince pie.

banger, *n.* (colloq.) 1. an old car, a clunker, equally onomatopoeic. 2. a sausage.

bang-on, *adj.* (colloq.) on the button; just what's needed. Not surprisingly, the term originated with World War II bomber crews.

bank holiday, *n.* public holiday.

B.A.O.R., *abbr.* British Army of the Rhine; the British troops in Germany.

bargee, *n.* a barge hand. It can also mean rough clothes such as might be worn by a barge hand.

barmy, *adj.* (colloq.) crazy. A working-class word.

barney, *n.* (colloq.) a quarrel, row.

baronet, *n.* a title of nobility ranking just below that of baron. A baronet's name is preceded by Sir, but unlike a knighthood, which also rates a Sir, a baronetcy is inherited. A baronet styles himself "Sir John Smith, bart." to distinguish himself from a knight.

barrack, *v.* to interrupt a speaker or performer with shouts or objections.

barrel organ, *n.* hurdy-gurdy.

barrister, *n.* a lawyer who pleads cases in court. The legal profession in Britain is divided into barristers and solicitors. The latter do mostly out-of-court work, though, under recent changes in the law, they are entitled to appear in most courts.

barrow, *n.* pushcart.

bash, *v.* and *n.,* to hit or smash. It also has a number of loose, colloquial meanings. To "have a bash" at something means to have a try; to "bash away" means to struggle on, and it can mean sexual intercourse.

basin, *n.* often, a bowl, as in pudding basin or washbasin.

bath, *v.* to have a bath.

Bath bun, *n.* a small, semi-sweet cake.

Bath-chair, *n.* a large wheelchair. Named after the city of Bath, a spa resort popular with invalids since the Roman occupation of Britain.

bathe, *v.* to go swimming, not to have a bath.

bathroom, *n.* just that. It may not have a toilet, which is often in a separate room by itself. If you want the toilet in Britain, it is better to say so.

batman, *n.* a senior army or air force officer's personal servant, also a soldier. The word predates Batman and has no connection with him.

batsman, *n.* the batter in cricket.

batten, *n.* a strip of wood.

beak, *n.* (colloq.) a magistrate, or a schoolteacher.

bearskin, *n.* the tall black fur hat worn by soldiers on ceremonial guard duty (see also **busby**).

bed-sitting room, *n.* a room let for a person to live in, or any room that serves as bedroom and living room. Sometimes shortened to **bed-sitter.**

Beefeater, *n.* a Yeoman of the Guard who patrols the Tower of London, resplendent in a scarlet uniform. The office is archaic.

beetle off, *v.* (colloq.) hurry away.

Mrs. Beeton, *n.* a cooking and household management book that is still a standby despite having been written nearly 100 years ago. Full of briskly practical advice and homilies as well as recipes, the book is known familiarly by the name of the authoress, e.g., "I looked it up in Mrs. Beeton."

beetroot, *n.* beet.

Belisha beacon, *n.* a pole with an orange ball on top that marks a pedestrian crossing point. Named after Leslie Hore-Belisha, the Minister of Transport who initiated them in 1937.

belt, *v.* (colloq.) to travel at speed.

belt up, *v.* shut up, stop talking.

bend, *n.* (colloq.) "round the bend" means crazy.

bent, *adj.* (colloq.) crooked. A police and underworld term, mostly.

berk, *n.* (colloq.) a stupid and disagreeable person. It is a mild term of abuse, though its derivation is obscene: from the rhyming slang phrase "Berkeley hunt." (See **rhyming slang.**)

bespoke, *adj.* custom-tailored.

big dipper, *n.* roller coaster.

big end, *n.* in a car, the larger end of the connecting rod.

bilberry, *n.* a native fruit similar to a blueberry.

bill, *n.* a restaurant or bar check, as well as a bill in a store. *Check* is not used for any kind of bill in Britain.

billiard table, *n.* a pool table. "Pool" is almost unknown in Britain.

Billingsgate, *prop. n.* foul, abusive language. Billingsgate is a London fish market where the bad language is proverbial, hence the expression "the tongue of a fishwife." It was so 300 years ago, it would seem from a snatch of dialogue from the seventeenth-century play *The Plain Dealer* by William Wycherley:

QUAINT: With sharp invectives—
WIDOW: Alias Billingsgate.

billion, *n.* 1,000,000 million; a thousand times as much as an American billion, which is written in Britain 1,000 million. The other powers are similarly different: a trillion is a million cubed, a quadrillion a million to the fourth power, and so on.

billycan, *n.* a can for boiling water, an item of camper's equipment. The word comes from Australia.

bind, *n.* (colloq.) a drag, an onerous task.

bint, *n.* (colloq.) girl. A disrespectful term, an Arabic word brought back by soldiers from the Middle East, where they regarded most girls with disrespect. Working-class.

bird, *n.* (colloq.) girl.

Biro, *n.* ball-point pen. A trade name that has become a generic term. Pronounced "by-roe."

biscuit, *n.* cookie or cracker.

bitter, *n.* the most widely-consumed kind of beer in Britain. (When you order beer in a pub, you always specify the kind: bitter, lager, light ale, or whatever. A Briton would no more ask simply for "beer" than he would ask in a restaurant for "meat.") A time-worn, bilingual joke:

Waiter in a Berlin cocktail lounge: *Bitte?*

British customer: No, whisky and soda, please.

black, *v.* a labor move which involves refusing to work on a product or place, usually in support of other strike action. If unions black a port, members will refuse to move cargoes into or out of it.

black, *n.* to "put up a black" means to commit an egregious error, to blot one's copybook.

Black and Tans, *n.* the British auxiliary police who carried out repressive measures in Ireland during the Anglo-Irish War of 1920–21, so called because of the color of their uniforms.

blackleg, *n.* a scab in a labor dispute.

blackshirt, *adj.* and *n.* fascist. The British Union of Fascists in the 1930s used to wear black shirts, after the style of Mussolini's followers.

blancmange, *n.* vanilla (or other flavored) pudding. Pronounced "blamonge."

blessed, *adj.* (colloq.) an all-purpose adjective, added for emphasis. Working-class.

Blighty, *n.* England. A World War I army term from the Hindi, which has lingered on.

blimey, *interj.* a mild exclamation, though it is descended, over the centuries, from the stronger "God blind me!" Cockney.

Blimp or **Colonel Blimp,** *prop.*

n. an archetypal mossback with old-fashioned, jingoistic, militaristic ideas.

blind, *v.* (colloq.) curse, swear, usually used in the phrase "effing and blinding."

block or **block of flats,** *n.* apartment house. The word *block* in the American sense (of a city block) does not exist in Britain.

block, *n.* a cut, in printing.

bloke, *n.* fellow, guy.

bloody, *adj.* (colloq.) an all-purpose adjective. It rarely has any specific meaning, though in upper-class speech it is occasionally used as a mildly vulgar synonym for "awful," as in "How perfectly bloody!" It can be attached to any noun for emphasis and, usually, to add a note of exasperation or annoyance, e.g., "The bloody train's late." It was once a fairly strong swear word, and when it was first spoken on the stage in Bernard Shaw's *Pygmalion,* audiences "trembled and shuddered," as a New York *Times* correspondent wrote at the time. But that was in 1912, and there are few places today where its use would cause any quivers. In the more genteel Britain that fought World War II, an official British pamphlet for American servicemen advised that "bloody" was best not used in mixed company, but was not forbidden to sol-diers in battle (there may have been a few GIs who missed the irony).

bloody-minded, *adj.* (colloq.) in a difficult mood, deliberately unhelpful.

blooming, *adj.* (colloq.) an all-purpose adjective, much like "bloody," but almost entirely working-class.

blower, *n.* 1. the private telephone lines that link a racetrack with off-track bookmakers. 2. (colloq.) a telephone.

blue, *v.* (colloq.) to spend money impetuously or quickly.

blue-eyed boy, *n.* fair-haired boy, favorite.

bob, *n.* (colloq.) shilling, the coin that is now, under decimal coinage, fivepence.

bobby, *n.* (colloq.) a policeman. The term derives from the name of the man who, as Home Secretary, created the modern British police forces in 1829, Sir Robert ("Bobby") Peel. Policemen used to be called "peelers" in the last century, and in Northern Ireland they are still.

boffin, *n.* a scientist or technologist. It came into use during World War II as service slang.

bog, *n.* (colloq.) toilet. Army and schoolboy slang.

boiler suit, *n.* overalls.

bolshie, *adj.* (colloq.) rebellious, refusing to conform or fall into line. An abbreviation of Bolshevik.

bolt hole, *n.* (colloq.) a safe hiding place.

bomb, *n.* (colloq.) 1. a great success, the exact opposite of its meaning in American. "It was a bomb!" means it was a hit (if a play) or a ball (if a party). It is also used, in a curious grammatical construction, with the verb "to go"; "It went a bomb" means it worked out great. The word is newish and used in the more modern occupations; it is more likely to be heard among advertising men or movie people than doctors or lawyers, at the Dorchester Bar more than the Reform Club. 2. a lot of money, e.g., "It cost a bomb."

Bombay duck, *n.* a tropical fish, the bummalo, usually eaten dried and served with a dish of curry.

bonce, *n.* (colloq.) head, brains. Cockney.

bonk, *v.* to hit. A lightweight word, which would not be used about a very serious episode.

bonkers, *adj.* (colloq.) crazy. It is used only as a predicate adjective, never before a noun, e.g., "He's bonkers," never "He's a bonkers chap."

bonnet, *n.* the hood of a car.

book, *v.* reserve, as book a table at a restaurant.

bookstall, *n.* a newsstand.

boot, *n.* the trunk of a car.

boozer, *n.* (colloq.) a pub, a drinking place, as often as a person who drinks.

Borstal, *n.* a prison school to which lawbreakers aged 16–19 can be sent as an alternative to jail.

bottom drawer, *n.* a hope chest.

bottom of the street *n.* end of the street.

bowler, *n.* derby hat. Also, in cricket, the man who throws the ball to the batsman.

bowls, *n.* a game similar to the Italian bocce, and quite unlike bowling, played with large balls on a flat lawn, mostly by elderly men.

box clever, *v.* to act shrewdly and cunningly.

Boxing Day, *n.* December 26th, a public holiday except in Scotland.

braces, *n.* suspenders (suspenders are "garters")

brambleberry, *n.* another, less common, word for blackberry.

Breathalyser, *n.* a device used by the police for analyzing the breath of people suspected of drunken driving.

breve, *n.* double whole note. Musical.

brew up, *v.* to make tea.

brigadier, *n.* brigadier general.

brilliant, *adj.* the $3\frac{1}{2}$-point type known in America as ruby.

brilliantine, *n.* a dressing that adds gloss to the hair.

broad bean, *n.* a bean resembling a lima bean, only harder.

Broadmoor, *n.* an institution for the criminally insane.

Broads, see **Norfolk Broads.**

brolly, *n.* (colloq.) short for umbrella.

brothel-creepers, *n.* (colloq.) men's shoes with thick crepe soles.

brouhaha, *n.* tumult, uproar.

brown ale, *n.* ale that is dark brown in color, a common pub drink.

browned-off, *adj.* (colloq.) fed up.

Brownies, *n.* the junior Girl Guides (Girl Scouts).

Brum (colloq.) Birmingham (England—the second largest city—not Alabama).

B.S.T., *n.* British Standard Time, roughly equivalent to Daylight Saving Time.

b.t.u., *n.* British thermal unit, a measure of heat.

bubble-and-squeak, *n.* meat and cabbage fried together, sometimes with potato.

budgerigar, *n.* an Australian parakeet. Sometimes shortened to "budgie." The commonest kind is kept as a pet.

buffer, *n.* the bumper at the end of a railroad track.

bugger, *v.* (colloq.) as well as its formal meaning, to commit sodomy, this is also a colloquial term that is less vulgar than one might suppose from its derivation, and as such has a number of meanings: 1. to foul up or render useless, e.g., "That's buggered our plan." 2. *bugger off*—scram, beat it.

3. in the passive tense, e.g., "I'm buggered," it means tired out, exhausted. 4. in the passive, "Well, I'll be buggered!" it can be a simple expletive like "Well, I'll be damned!"

bugger, *n.* (colloq.) 1. a person, not necessarily in any pejorative sense. 2. an awful situation. A man in a pub talking about a colleague who had just lost his job said, "Being out of work with a wife pregnant is a bugger!" 3. A homosexual. In this sense, very old-fashioned, though still heard occasionally.

bugger-all, see **all.**

building society, *n.* a loan society that provides mortgages.

bukshee, see **bakshee.**

bull, *n.* rigid and unnecessary military discipline.

bullet, *n.* (colloq.) the sack from a job.

bum, *n.* (colloq.) ass, rectum. This word goes back at least 500 years, but over the past ten its use among adults has dwindled as the American meaning takes over, though schoolchildren still use it. At least there are not so many puerile jokes now about the confusion of the two meanings.

bumf, *n.* (colloq.) documentation. Though many people who use the word blithely don't realize it, it comes from an old army term, "bumfodder," meaning usable as toilet paper (see **bum**).

bummaree, *n.* a porter in a fish market.

bun, *n.* a soft, sweet roll, halfway to being a cake, usually eaten with butter.

bun-fight, *n.* (colloq.) a humorous term for a tea party or other social occasion.

bung, *v.* (colloq.) throw, toss.

Burton, *n.* a kind of beer, named for the town where it is brewed. In R.A.F. slang, to "go for a Burton" means to be killed. Sometimes it is used to mean a thing is broken, as in "My watch has gone for a Burton."

busby, *n.* a tall fur hat with a bag hanging from the top, worn by Hussars in the British Army. It is used commonly to describe the tall black fur hats worn by the soldiers on ceremonial guard duty outside the royal palaces, but the army will not accept this term for them, and calls these "bearskins."

bushel, *n.* 2,219 cubic inches, against an American bushel's 2,150 cubic inches.

busker, *n.* street musician.

butchers, *n.* (colloq.) a look at something as in "Let's have a butchers at it." Rhyming slang (butcher's hook).

butter-up, *v.* (colloq.) to sweet-talk, flatter.

butty, *n.* (colloq.) sandwich. Mostly Northern and working-class.

buzz-off, *v.* (colloq.) scram.

by-law, *n.* municipal ordinance.

by-word, *n.* household word, often standing for something, as in "his name was a by-word for dishonesty."

cack-handed, *adj.* (colloq.) clumsy.

cadge, *v.* to borrow or beg.

café, *n.* a cheap restaurant or snack bar, a "greasy spoon." Usually pronounced "caff."

cake-hole, *n.* (colloq.) mouth.

call-up, *n.* draft. "Nixon pledges to end call-up by next July"— London *Times* headline, August 29, 1972.

camp bed, *n.* cot. A cot in Britain is a bed for a small child.

cannabis, *n.* marijuana. This is the official and the most common newspaper term for it, but it does not replace "pot."

Cantabrian, *prop. n.* and *adj.* a graduate of Cambridge University, or, as an adjective, referring to Cambridge.

canvasser, *n.* someone who solicits votes for a candidate, or takes a poll on behalf of one.

caravan, *n.* trailer.

card punch, *n.* key punch.

cards, *n.* (colloq.) in common parlance, one's cards are one's National Insurance papers, held by an employer, who has to put a weekly stamp on them signifying payment of his contribution. When a workman is "given his cards," he is fired.

caretaker, *n.* janitor.

Carey Street, *prop. n.* (colloq.)

the location of the bankruptcy court in London; hence, to be "in Carey Street" is to be bankrupt. (One is *in* a street in Britain, not on it.)

car park, *n.* parking lot.

carriage, *n.* railroad or subway car.

carrier bag, *n.* shopping bag.

carve-up, *n.* a swindle perpetrated by a number of people.

cashier, *n.* teller.

castor sugar, *n.* very fine granulated sugar.

catapult, *n.* slingshot.

catch up, *v.* overtake.

caucus, *n.* a permanent group within a political party. This word changed meaning slightly when it crossed over from America.

C.B.E., *prop. n.* Companion of the British Empire, a title awarded for services to the community.

cellarman, *n.* a man who works behind the scenes in a pub.

centenary, *n.* centennial. Pronounced "centinnary."

central reservation, *n.* divider on a road.

certified, *adj.* in common parlance, certified insane.

chambers, *n.* a lawyer's office.

champers, *n.* (colloq.) champagne. This is an upper-class usage, in which the suffix "er" is added to the first syllable of a word. Eric Partridge, in his *Dictionary of Slang and Unconventional English,* says it began at Oxford in 1875 and came out of there with the bright young things in the 1920s. Occasionally, this is applied to ordinary words, e.g., "preggers"—pregnant—but more often to a name, to denote easy familiarity. Thus, the gamblers' swank Clermont Club, owned by John Aspinall, is known in some circles as "Aspers," and among Britons all over the Far East, the local branch of the Hong Kong and Shanghai Bank is the "Honkers and Shankers."

Chancellor of the Duchy of Lancaster, *prop. n.* an archaic post often given to someone of real political importance to give him a seat in the cabinet (also see **Lord Privy Seal**). For instance, when Geoffrey Rippon negotiated Britain's entry into the European Economic Community, this was his only official post.

Chancellor of the Exchequer, *prop. n.* the cabinet minister equivalent to the Secretary of the Treasury.

Channel, *prop. n.* the English Channel.

chapel, *n.* any Nonconformist church (see **Nonconformist**). Also, as in America, a small place of worship of any Christian denomination.

char, 1. *v.* to do menial housework for someone else. The word is a corruption of "chore." 2. *n.* a person paid to do housework; also **charlady. 3.** *n.* (colloq.) tea. Working-class.

charabanc, *n.* a long-distance sight-seeing bus.

charge hand, *n.* the head of a crew of workmen.

charge sheet, *n.* the police blotter.

charlie, *n.* (colloq.) a fool.

cheesed-off, *adj.* fed up, annoyed.

chemin de fer, *n.* a card game, a favorite with British gamblers, imported from France, and pronounced the French way. Sometimes shortened in speech to "shemmy."

chemist, *n.* a druggist. A chemist's shop is a drugstore, but it sells a much more limited range of goods than an American drugstore, and has no soda fountain.

Chequers, *prop. n.* the Prime Minister's official country residence.

chesterfield, *n.* a heavily padded sofa.

chicory, *n.* endive.

Chiltern Hundreds, *prop. n.* the Stewardship of the Chiltern Hundreds is an archaic and by now almost mythical office, which is traditionally incompatible with being a Member of Parliament. If a member wants to resign, he does so by applying for the Stewardship of the Chiltern Hundreds, which is automatically granted him.

chimney, *n.* smokestack. (But on a ship a smokestack is a funnel.)

Chindits, *prop. n.* an elite and much-admired force that fought behind the Japanese lines in Burma in World War II.

chipolata, *n.* a skinny sausage.

chips, *n.* French fried potatoes.

chit, *n.* (colloq.) pass, document, or other piece of paper. Originally a service slang word, and like many others, stemming from a Hindi word that the army brought back from India.

chivvy, *v.* to prod, press someone for action.

choked, *adj.* (colloq.) angry, resentful. Working-class.

choker, *n.* neckerchief or scarf. A working-class term, though it was once high fashion.

Christmas box, *n.* a Christmas present, usually one given on Boxing Day to someone who provides service, such as a janitor or milkman.

Christmas pudding, *n.* plum pudding.

chuck, *v.* to throw. **chuck it,** *v.* (colloq.) to stop, desist, call it off.

chuck or **chuck steak,** *n.* pieces of stewing meat.

chucker-out, *n.* bouncer.

chuffed, *adj.* (colloq.) pleased.

church warden, *n.* a lay official of a Church of England parish.

churn, *n.* a large milk can as well as a butter-making machine.

chutney, *n.* a popular Indian condiment of spices and other ingredients, or the domestic imitation.

C.I.D., *prop. n.* Criminal Investigation Department, the plain-clothes branch of a police force.

circus, *n.* an important intersection of several streets, usually roughly circular. Picadilly Circus is a London landmark.

City, *prop. n.* the old City of London, or the financial world of which it is the center. "Opinion in the City" means the same thing that "opinion on Wall Street" would mean in America. The sentence "He's something in the City" means he is a financial executive.

city editor, *n.* the financial editor of a newspaper.

civil list, *n.* the system by which Parliament provides money for the royal household and certain old retainers.

civvy street, *n.* (colloq.) civilian life. A service term.

cladding, *n.* a covering of any kind on a structure, e.g., "wood cladding on bathroom walls."

clanger, *n.* a conspicuous mistake, a resounding gaffe.

clapped-out, *adj.* (colloq.) worn out, exhausted.

clippie, *n.* (colloq.) a woman ticket collector on a bus.

clobber, *n.* (colloq.) kit, tools, and equipment, or else clothes for the job.

close, *adj.* a description of the weather, meaning heavy, humid, still, and stifling.

clot, *n.* (colloq.) a fool. The word is of the 1940s, and today has a period flavor about it.

clotted cream, *n.* very thick cream, a specialty of Devon and Cornwall.

coach, *n.* a long-distance bus.

cobblers, *n.* (colloq.) balls, testicles, as in "That's a lot of cobblers."

cock, *n.* (colloq.) a familiar form of address to a man, as in "Hello, old cock."

cockle, *n.* a tiny edible shellfish, sold by the half-pint from push-carts, an old-fashioned trade that is dying out slowly. ("Cockles and mussels, alive, alive-o," as the old street cry and the song have it.)

Cockney, *n.* and *adj.* a working-class accent and argot found mostly in East London, or the person who uses it. In the rest of Britain, a Cockney is any working-class Londoner. By tradition, a Cockney is someone born within the sound of Bow Bells (the bells of St. Mary-le-Bow Church) .

cock-up, *n.* (colloq.) a mess, a fouled-up situation. Rather vulgar.

cod, *n.* and *adj.* joke, spoof, or parody. A sophisticated word.

codswollop, *n.* (colloq.) nonsense.

cold, *adj.* not warm. If you ask for cold water/milk/beer, it will come cold, but not iced. If you want it ice-cold, you must say so.

coley, *n.* rock salmon or cod.

college, *n.* 1. an institute of higher education that does not have the status of a university or award a degree. 2. a school within the university at Oxford, Cambridge or London universities. 3. some public (private) schools that style themselves colleges.

Colonel Blimp, see **Blimp.**

combinations, *n.* union suit, long johns.

come-uppance, *n.* just deserts, as in "He got his come-uppance."

comforter, *n.* scarf.

commissionaire, *n.* uniformed doorman.

commis waiter, *n.* busboy. A **commis chef** is an assistant chef.

common, *n.* a piece of public parkland.

common, *adj.* lower-class. The word reeks of uptight, middle-class snobbery, and is given its place by Noel Coward in some sentiments he puts into a woman's mouth in his play *Fumed Oak:* "She's common for one thing, she dyes her hair for another, and she's a bit too free and easy all round for my taste."

commoner, *n.* anyone who is not of noble rank.

common-or-garden, *adj.* ordinary, standard model. The term comes from gardening catalogues.

compère, *n.* master of ceremonies.

compositor, *n.* typesetter.

comprehensive school, *n.* a high school that includes both the more and less educationally advanced pupils, unlike most schools, which take one or the other.

concert party, *n.* a vaudeville (music hall) show put on at some place other than a regular theater, i.e., a park, seafront promenade, summer camp.

conk, *n.* (colloq.) nose.

conker, *n.* the hard brown nut inside a chestnut bur. British schoolboys collect these and play a game with them called conkers.

conk-out, *v.* (colloq.) to break down, stop working.

Conservative, *prop. n.* a member of the Conservative Party, one of the two major political parties. This does not imply being as far to the right as it would in America.

Consols, *n.* the financial world's term for the British Government's consolidated annuities.

constable, *n.* an ordinary policeman. (See also **P.C.**) A police chief is a **Chief Constable.**

consultant, *n.* the senior rank of doctor in a hospital.

Continent, *prop. n.* the phrase "the Continent" always means the European continent, as distinct from the British Isles. Continental usually refers to this, but lately has come to be also a euphemism referring to Indian and Pakistani immigrants. A store advertising Continental food may mean either one.

convenience, *n.* public toilet.

conversion, *n.* a house converted into separate apartments.

conversion heater, *n.* electric heater.

conveyancing, *n.* the legal arrangements for the transfer of a piece of property.

cooker, *n.* stove, oven.

cookery book, *n.* cookbook.

cop, *v.* (colloq.) to get something unpleasant, e.g., "He copped a five-pound fine." In service slang, to "cop it" sometimes means to be killed.

copper-bottomed, *adj.* (colloq.) sound, thorough. I've heard talk of "copper-bottomed shares" and "a copper-bottomed bastard."

cop shop, *n.* (colloq.) police station.

copy taster, *n.* a person on a newspaper who looks at incoming copy and decides what should be done with it.

cords, *n.* (colloq.) corduroy pants.

corn, *n.* all edible grains.

corned beef, *n.* processed meat. American-style corned beef is called "salt beef."

cornet, *n.* cone, as in "ice cream cornet."

corn flour, *n.* cornstarch.

corporation, *n.* a municipal government. People who work for the municipality are "corporation employees."

cosh, *n.* a club, or stick shaped into a weapon. Also a verb, **to cosh**—to hit with a club.

cos lettuce, *n.* romaine lettuce.

coster or **coster-monger,** *n.* someone who sells things from a pushcart.

cot, *n.* a crib for a very small child, usually a small bed with sides. A "crib" in British is for a newborn baby only. A "cot" (American) is a camp bed.

cotton wool, *n.* absorbent cotton.

council flat or **council house,** *n.* an apartment or house rented from the local authority, often at a subsidized price. Characteristically, working-class housing.

counsel, *n.* a barrister retained by a solicitor to plead a case in court.

county family, *n.* an old-established, upper-class landowning country family. **County** (*adj.*) also refers to the life style.

county school, *n.* a public school (in the American rather than the British sense) coming under a local council, usually in a rural area.

courtesy title, *n.* a title given by custom rather than heraldic right, such as the titles given to many of the children of the nobility. For instance, the eldest son of a duke is styled "The Marquess of—" (his father's second title) and all the children of a viscount or baron are called "the honorable."

Coventry, *prop. n.* if someone is "sent to Coventry" it means that people refuse to talk to him.

crackers, *adj.* (colloq.) crazy. But, like **bonkers,** it is never used descriptively before a noun.

cracking, *v.* (colloq.) to "get cracking" means to get moving, to take vigorous action, get on with the job.

Cranwell, *n.* the Royal Air Force academy.

crib, *n.* 1. a crib, but one for a newborn baby only. After that, the infant sleeps in a slightly larger bed, which is called a cot. 2. in school or college, a pony, something from which answers to an exam can be copied.

crib, *v.* to copy, usually illicitly.

crisps, *n.* potato chips.

crock, *n.* an old car or, facetiously, an aged and infirm person, e.g., "I've got a backache again today; I'll be a real old crock soon."

croft, *n.* a small farm in Scotland. A **crofter** farms one.

crotchet, *n.* a quarter note in music.

Crown estate, *n.* lands owned by the nation.

cruet, *n.* a set of containers for condiments at the table, usually salt, pepper, and mustard. It does not mean a bottle, as in America.

Cruft's, *prop. n.* the annual dog show in London, named after the founder, Charles Cruft. A national event in Britain.

crumpet, *n.* 1. a flat roll for toasting. 2. (colloq.) sex, or a girl available as a sexual partner. There are many old vaudeville sketches around this double entendre, typically with a white-moustached colonel sitting on a colonial verandah saying that now he's had his tea he feels like some crumpet.

CS gas, *n.* the riot gas used by British security forces, similar to Mace in its effects.

Cup Final, *n.* the biggest soccer match of the season, for the national championship.

cupboard, *n.* closet; "closet" dropped out of use in Britain a couple of centuries ago; a remnant is w.c. (for "water closet") meaning toilet.

cuppa, *n.* (colloq.) cup of tea.

curate, *n.* an assistant vicar.

currant loaf, *n.* loaf of raisin bread.

current account, *n.* checking account, at the bank.

curriculum vitae, *n.* a résumé of one's career, such as is sent with a job application.

cushy, *adj.* (colloq.) easy, soft. Originally a wartime term.

cutting, *n.* clipping, in the press or horticultural sense, e.g., a clipping from a newspaper or a clipping from a bush.

cut-throat, *n.* (colloq.) an open-bladed, or straight, razor.

cut-up, *adj.* upset, as in "He's very

cut-up about it." Upper-class, and with a stiff-upper-lip tone.

Dame, *n.* a title conferred on a woman, equivalent to a knighthood.

damn-all, *n.* (colloq.) absolutely nothing. See all.

Darby and Joan, *prop. n.* the archetypal elderly, happily married couple. There are Darby and Joan Clubs in many localities.

Dartmouth, *prop. n.* the Royal Naval College, equivalent to Annapolis.

davenport, *n.* an antique folding writing desk.

dead, *adj.* (colloq.) very. Cockney.

de-bag, *v.* to take the pants off someone as a joke (see **bags**).

Debrett's Peerage, *n.* the standard bloodstock and heraldic guide to British nobility and their lineage. It is accurate so far as possible, and technically, at least, undeserving of Oscar Wilde's oft-quoted crack, put into the mouth of one of the characters in his play *A Woman of No Importance:* "You should study the peerage, Gerald . . . . It's the best thing in fiction that the English have ever done."

decorator, *n.* a house painter and paperhanger.

decree nisi, *n.* a divorce decree that becomes effective ("absolute" in British legal parlance)

only after a stated period, usually three months. This allows time for the court to rescind it if it seems that the terms, such as financial ones, are not being complied with.

deed poll, *n.* a legal declaration of intention, most commonly used in changing one's name.

dekko, *n.* (colloq.) a look, a glimpse. A word brought back from the Orient.

demerara, *n.* a brown sugar from the West Indies, used for coffee.

demo, *n.* (colloq.) a common abbreviation of "demonstration," in the political sense.

demob, *n.* and *v.* (colloq.) discharge from the services. From "demobilize."

deposit account, *n.* savings account at a bank.

detached, *adj.* of a house, separated from the buildings on either side. **Semi-detached** means separated on one side and joined on the other; in Britain, houses are often built in tandem. **Semi** is a common term for a semi-detached house.

dicey, *adj.* (colloq.) risky, uncertain.

dicky seat, *n.* rumble seat, if anyone remembers what that is.

diddle, *v.* (colloq.) gyp.

digestive biscuit, *n.* a soft, wholemeal cookie.

digs, *n.* furnished lodgings. Also, occasionally, **diggings.**

dim, *adj.* stupid, thick-headed. An

American would say "dim-witted." A famous poem by Reginald Reynolds attacking nuclear war preparations, and parodying a well-known patriotic poem, began:

Breathes there a soul so bloody dim
It does not once occur to him
When some mass suicide is planned,
"This is my own, my native land."

dinner jacket, *n.* tuxedo.

direct grant school, *n.* a private school that receives a subsidy from the local government with the proviso that it takes a number of pupils without fees.

directly, *adj.* immediately. Used much less than it was.

director, *n.* a member of the governing board of a business corporation (or limited company, in British terminology). A director of a company may take no part in the day-to-day running of it. One who does is often called an **executive director.**

directory enquiries, *n.* (on the telephone) information. If you want to know a number, you ask for this.

dispensary, *n.* the department of a chemist's (drugstore) or hospital that makes up and dispenses medicines.

district commissioner, *n.* a government official in a colonial territory with powers to enforce law and adjudicate disputes.

divider, *n.* central strip on a road dividing two directions of traffic.

do, *n.* (colloq.) a party or other social function. More broadly, it can sometimes mean any arranged event involving a number of people: I have heard a bloody commando raid described as a "dicey do."

do, *v.* (colloq.) 1. to get, in an aggressive sense, as in "I'll do you." In this sense, it is often used jokingly. 2. to cheat. Used mostly, though not exclusively, in the passive mood, as in "I've been done."

do for, *v.* to clean up and keep house for someone. If a bachelor has someone coming in a few times a week to clean up and cook, she will say, "I do for him."

do in, *v.* (colloq.) kill.

doddle, *n.* (colloq.) a pushover, something easy. Cockney.

dodge, *n.* a shrewd and artful expedient.

dodgem car, *n.* bumper car in a fairground.

dodgy, *adj.* (colloq.) risky, or questionable in some way, often legally.

dogsbody, *n.* (colloq.) someone who does the odd jobs that no one else wants to do.

doings, *n.* (colloq.) a thingamajig.

dole, *n.* welfare payments to an unemployed person.

dollar, *n.* (colloq.) 25 new pence. This dates back to pre–World War II, when a dollar was worth 5 shillings.

28

dollop, *n.* a large serving.

dolly-girl, *n.* a young and pretty girl, by implication long on sex appeal and short on brains. A newish term.

don, *n.* a member of the teaching staff of a university.

doodah, *n.* a thingamajig.

doolally, *adj.* (colloq.) weak in the head.

dormitory, *n.* a room in which a lot of people sleep, as in a boarding school. It does not mean a building, as in American. An American college teacher was talking to a British counterpart in England recently and remarked that at his college, male and female undergraduates now sleep in the same dormitory. "Ye gods!" said the Englishman, and they talked at cross-purposes for some time.

doss house, *n.* flophouse.

dotty, *adj.* crazy or zany. A genteel term, usually used flippantly.

double cream, *n.* heavy whipping cream.

doughnut, *n.* a round, sweet pastry, with sugar on the outside and jam inside. It is quite different from an American doughnut.

DPP, *prop. n.* the Director of Public Prosecutions, the Government official who is the final arbiter on whether or not someone is prosecuted for an alleged offense. If a coroner or other official wants to bring the possibility that a crime has been committed to official attention, he contacts the DPP's office.

dram, *n.* a drink of whisky. It was originally a measure.

draper, *n.* a person who sells cloth and certain clothes.

draughts, *n.* checkers.

drawing pin, *n.* a thumbtack.

dress down, *v.* tell off, bawl out.

dresser, *n.* kitchen sideboard.

dressing gown, *n.* bathrobe.

dropsy, *n.* (colloq.) a bribe, meaning something dropped in the pocket.

dual carriageway, *n.* divided highway.

duck, *n.* a score of zero in cricket, sometimes used in other situations.

ducks, *n.* 1. white flannels. 2. (colloq.) a term of endearment.

dumb, *n.* mute, bereft of speech. It does not usually mean stupid. The English writer Edward Shanks once wrote in an article in the London *Evening Standard* about his travels in America that he was startled to hear someone say: "My sister Annabelle is dumb; she never stops talking."

dummy, *n.* baby's pacifier.

dust cover or **dust jacket,** *n.* book cover.

dustman, *n.* garbage collector.

dust-up, *n.* (colloq.) fight, row.

Dutch courage, *n.* courage inspired by alcohol. Walter Scott has the hero of *Redgauntlet,* facing a daunting romantic entanglement, push aside liquor with the words: "Not a drop. No Dutch courage for me."

each-way, *adj.* a bet on a horse to win, place, or show.

early closing, *n.* the day of the week in each district in which the local stores close at lunchtime, to give the people who work in them a half-day off. "Savannah has all the pace of an English village during early closing." Richard Neville in the London *Evening Standard,* July 20, 1972.

earnest, *n.* a promise, or at least an indication, of what is to follow. Used often in legal correspondence, e.g., "We are sending you a deposit as an earnest of our intention to proceed with this matter."

earth wire, *n.* ground wire.

East Anglia, *prop. n.* the area of eastern England that bulges out into the North Sea.

East End, *prop. n.* the part of London containing most of the older poorer neighborhoods. (See also **West End.**)

Eccles cake, *n.* a flat cake with a filling of dried fruit and spice.

egg flip, *n.* eggnog.

eiderdown, *n.* quilt, comforter.

elastic band, *n.* rubber band.

eleven-plus, *n.* an exam taken by many schoolchildren at the age of 11 to determine which of two streams of secondary education each will enter.

elevenses, *n.* a midmorning snack.

Employment Exchange, *n.* the modern name for the government-run office which tries to find work for unemployed people. Most people still call it by the old name, **Labour Exchange.**

engaged, *n.* busy, tied-up. On the telephone, "The number is engaged" means the line is busy.

enjoin, *v.* to compel, to order by law; the exact opposite of the usual American meaning.

erk, *n.* (colloq.) the lowest rank in the air force or navy.

esquire, *n.* a form of written address, in formal or polite correspondence, added after the name of a man who does not have any title or rank. Mr. John Smith becomes "John Smith, Esq." (the word is not written in full). However, Lord Smith or Major John Smith would not add an Esq. Originally, the term denoted status, and only a member of the property-owning class rated it. But in the age of the common man, hierarchical distinctions are reduced, and everyone gets something before or after his name, as at a children's party where there are competitive games but everybody gets some kind of prize.

estate car, *n.* station wagon.

ex-directory, *adj.* unlisted, of a telephone number.

express, *n.* special delivery; a postal term.

ex-serviceman, *n.* veteran. The

word "veteran" in British implies old age. A vet is a veterinary surgeon.

fag, 1. *n.* (colloq.) cigarette. 2. *n.* (colloq.) a dreary or onerous task. 3. *n.* at some public schools (in the British sense) a boy assigned to an older boy to be his part-time servant. (See **fag** in the American/British section.)

family allowance, *n.* a weekly payment by the Government to every family for a second child and any following.

fancy, *v.* want or like, as in "Do you fancy her?" and "He fancies himself," both common expressions.

fancy goods, *n.* small, decorative objects: the term is used mostly by stores.

fanlight, *n.* transom.

fanny, *n.* vagina. Vulgar. Actually the word is almost archaic, but is included here as a warning against using the American word. It came into use in the eighteenth century, after John Cleland's bawdy novel *Fanny Hill—Memoirs of a Woman of Pleasure.*

Father Christmas, *prop. n.* Santa Claus. Both terms are used.

fiddle, *v.* and *n.* (colloq.) cheat, gyp. A lightweight word that does not usually carry a tone of serious condemnation. As a verb, it takes an impersonal predicate, i.e., "He fiddled his

expenses," not "He fiddled the boss."

fire, *n.* a gas or electric heater.

fire brigade, *n.* fire department.

first, *n.* at university a degree with first-class honors.

first floor, *n.* second floor. The British and Europeans start counting floors one above the ground, which is always called the ground floor, so that what Americans call the second floor Britons call the first, and so on.

First Sea Lord, *prop. n.* commander of the navy, equivalent to the U.S. Chief of Naval Operations.

fishmonger's, *n.* fish store.

fixture, *n.* a schedule of sporting or other events.

fixtures and fittings or **f. and f.,** *n.* the nonmovable furnishing in an apartment, such as lights and built-in furniture, plus things not easily transferrable, such as carpets, draperies, etc. These are often sold with the transfer of an apartment. Since it is illegal to ask key money, the price for f. and f. is often in reality the price paid for the privilege of renting an apartment.

flakers, *adj.* (colloq.) tired, flaked-out (see **champers** for the significance of the "ers" ending). Upper-class. Another form is **Harry Flakers,** e.g., "I'm Harry Flakers tonight."

flan, *n.* an open pie.

flannel, 1. *n.* washcloth. 2. *n.* and *v.* (colloq.) half-truths or untruths designed to cover up something, soft soap. As a verb, it means to dish out soft soap.

flasher, *n.* (colloq.) an exhibitionist, in the sexual sense.

flat, *n.* apartment.

flautist, *n.* flutist.

flea pit, *n.* a shabby building, especially a movie theater.

Fleet Street, *prop. n.* the center of London's newspaper district; hence, national newspaper journalism. "He's landed a job in Fleet Street" does not describe the location of his office but the nature of the job.

flex, *n.* electric wire.

flibbertigibbet, *n.* a flighty, mercurial girl; though historically it means an imp or impish person, and could be applied to a male.

flicks, *n.* (colloq.) the movies.

flimsy, *n.* a sheet of thin typing paper, or a copy of something on one.

flipping, *adj.* (colloq.) an all-purpose adjective added for emphasis, mostly working-class. Clearly a euphemism.

flog, *v.* (colloq.) to sell.

fluid ounce, *n.* 1.73 cubic inches, against 1.80 cubic inches in an American fluid ounce.

flutter, *n.* a small bet.

fly, *adj.* shrewd, wily, knowing the angles, perhaps dishonest.

flyover, *n.* overpass.

football, *n.* soccer.

forces, *n.* the armed services.

form, *n.* 1. a class or grade at school, the nth form rather than the nth grade. 2. in horse racing, a horse's track record. 3. as a colloquial extension of 2, in underworld language it means criminal record.

fortnight, *n.* two weeks.

founder member, *n.* charter member.

Fred Karno's Army, *prop. n.* (colloq.) any military unit of comic ineffectiveness; after a famous vaudeville act of the 1900s. It was coined in World War I and first used by British soldiers about themselves, self-mockingly. Troops who were to fight heroically marched off singing a song that began:

> We are Fred Karno's Army
> The ragtime infantry.
> We cannot shoot, we cannot fight,
> What bloody use are we . . .

Free Churches, *prop. n.* nonconformist churches, Protestant churches in Britain other than the Church of England.

freehold, *adj.* used about property, it means without any legal encumbrances. "For sale freehold" means available for outright purchase.

french polish, *n.* a high-gloss polish used on furniture.

fridge, *n.* (colloq.) short for refrigerator.

fringe, *n.* bangs.

F.R.S., *abbr.* Fellow of the Royal Society, one of the highest honors that can be conferred on a British scientist.

full stop, *n.* period.

funk, *n.* fright. "In a blue funk" means terrified. **funk hole,** *n.* safe place in time of danger.

funnel, *n.* the smokestack on a ship.

gaffer, *n.* (colloq.) boss. Working-class.

gallon, *n.* 277.42 cubic inches, against an American gallon's 231 cubic inches (liquid).

game, *n.* (colloq.) prostitution. "On the game" means working as a hooker.

gammon, *n.* thick cuts of ham, usually served with vegetables as a meat course, or the meatiest cuts of bacon.

gammy, *adj.* (colloq.) unfit or injured, of a limb, e.g., "He's got a gammy leg."

ganger, *n.* the foreman of a gang of workmen; a straw boss.

garden, *n.* any plot of ground that is cultivated, or adjoins a house. Most Americans' yards would be gardens in England. Britons call it a yard only if it is paved with concrete.

gas, *v.* (colloq.) to talk emptily. Rather upper-class.

gash, *n.* spare parts or, more often, leftover bits and pieces which can serve as spares.

gasometer, *n.* a gas storage tank.

gateau, *n.* a rich cake. A Gallicism often used, particularly by people selling them.

gazump, *v.* to raise the price of property after someone has agreed to buy it. The term has only recently come into use. It comes from an archaic colloquial term "gazumph," to swindle, which in turn comes from the Yiddish.

G.C.E., *n.* General Certificate of Education, one of a series of certificates for passing exam stages, usually at ages 15–17.

gear, *n.* clothes. A newish, youthful term.

gearing, *n.* what Wall Street calls leverage; the ratio in a company between capital and money that is borrowed. A financial term.

gear lever, *n.* gearshift.

geezer, *n.* (colloq.) a bloke, a guy, usually odd in some way. See also **geyser.**

gelignite, *n.* an explosive made from nitroglycerin, nitrocotton, potassium acid, and wood pulp, much used in mining, for safe-blowing, and by the I.R.A.

gen, *n.* and *v.* (colloq.) information. It comes from the services, where it was an abbreviation of "intelligence." It is also used as a verb: "I'll gen you up on the situation" means "I'll fill you in." "Genned up" means well informed. A baroque use of the word that's heard occasionally is to "de-gen," meaning to extract information from someone.

general factotum, *n.* someone who does general duties.

gentry, *n.* ladies and gentlemen of good breeding. In bygone days, it meant specifically the class of landowners ranking just below the nobility.

Geordie, *prop. n.* (colloq.) someone from Tyneside, the River Tyne area in northeast England with Newcastle at its center.

George Cross, *prop. n.* a medal awarded for civilian bravery.

geyser, *n.* a gas-operated device for heating water, pronounced "geezer." It also refers to the natural phenomenon.

ghoulies, *n.* (colloq.) testicles. Upper-class, boarding school and service slang. "He thought of what Lord Canteloupe had told him over dinner at White's the previous day: 'When it comes down to brass tacks, one's better off working with shits. They'll kick you in the ghoulies as soon as look at you, but one knows that and can be ready for it. It's those chaps who have scruples that really kill you dead.'" From *Friends in Low Places* by Simon Raven. This puts the word accurately in its social setting.

giggle, *n.* (colloq.) a lark, something done just for fun. A Cockney term, but one of many that have been taken up by showbiz in its proletarianization of manners.

gillie, *n.* an assistant to someone out hunting game, who loads his shotgun for him. A Scottish word.

gilt-edged, *adj.* refers to Government stocks.

gin, *n.* a small trap for animals.

ginger or **ginger up,** *v.* to prod into further action. Also used adjectivally; within a large organization, such as a political party, a group of people will sometimes form a "ginger group."

ginger wine, *n.* a British-made, ginger-flavored wine.

Girl Guide, *n.* Girl Scout.

Giro, *n.* a banking system run by the Post Office.

git, *n.* (colloq.) person; a vaguely offensive term. Robert Graves says in his short book *Lars Porsena or the Future of Swearing* that it comes from "whore's git," or "whore's begat," but in recent years it has lost much of its strength.

glasshouse, *n.* (colloq.) a military prison.

glaze, *v.* to fit with glass, as a window. **glazier,** *n.* a person who fits windows.

glow worm, *n.* lightning bug.

gnomes of Zurich, *n.* the international Swiss bankers who supposedly pull strings and manipulate the international monetary system. They figure in British political folklore.

gods, *n.* (colloq.) the cheapest seats at the theater, at the back of the top balcony; so called because they are supposedly close to heaven.

goggle box, *n.* (colloq.) television set.

golden handshake, *n.* a financial

payment made to an executive on leaving a firm.

gong, *n.* (colloq.) medal or decoration. Originally service slang.

goods, *n.* freight, as in goods train, goods lift (elevator), etc.

goolies, see **ghoulies.**

Gorbals, *prop. n.* a notoriously rough slum district of Glasgow.

gorblimey! *interj.* an expression of surprise. It is Cockney, so much so that I've heard someone called "a real gorblimey Cockney." It derives from the archaic and blasphemous "God blind me!"

gormless, *adj.* (colloq.) stupid and unattractive.

governor, *n.* 1. the warden of a prison. 2. (colloq.) boss. Working-class.

governor-general, *n.* the Queen's representative in a dominion who signs laws and carries out ceremonials in her place.

G.P.O., *prop. n.* General Post Office.

gradient, *n.* grade on a road.

graft, *n.* (colloq.) 1. hard work, honest toil. 2. alternatively, almost the opposite, sharp dealings, such as dishonest sales talk. **grafter,** *n.* (colloq.) can be someone who practices either one.

gramophone, *n.* phonograph. The term is being replaced by "record player."

grammar school, *n.* the more advanced academically of the two kinds of schools into which much of British secondary education is divided, covering roughly the equivalent of sixth to twelfth grades. (See also **secondary modern school.**)

grass, *v.* (colloq.) to inform on someone. Mostly underworld.

greaseproof paper, *n.* waxed paper.

Green Cross Code, *n.* the road safety rules that schoolchildren learn.

green fingers, *n.* green thumbs.

greengage, *n.* a fruit similar to a plum, only green in color.

greengrocer, *n.* someone who sells fruits and vegetables, but not other staple foods. A grocer sells these and perhaps fruits and vegetables as well, as in America.

green paper, *n.* a statement of Government views or proposals, published as a document for discussion. (See also **white paper.**)

greens, *n.* green vegetables.

grind, *n.* (colloq.) sexual intercourse. " 'A good grind, eh?' said the tramp, looking after the fraulein."—from *Love Among the Haystacks* by D. H. Lawrence.

gripewater, *n.* a type of medicine commonly given to babies to help with digestion.

grizzle, *v.* to whine or cry complainingly.

grog, *n.* rum and water. Until 1971, a daily ration of grog was given to enlisted men in the

Royal Navy. It is used occasionally as a synonym for any liquor.

grotty, *adj.* (colloq.) shabby, run-down, or otherwise inferior. Not too serious. A new word that sprang up among young people in the Beatles era, it stems from "grotesque."

ground floor, *n.* first floor.

group-captain, *n.* an R.A.F. rank equivalent to colonel.

Grub Street, *prop. n.* the old name of a London street that used to be the home of impoverished authors and literary hacks. Now it refers to such people.

Guards, *prop. n.* the army division consisting of the five regiments which mount guard outside the Queen's palaces, plus two cavalry regiments which ride in royal processions. These are all fighting units, which perform their palace duties on a rotational system.

gubbins, *n.* thingamajig.

guinea, *n.* in pre-1971, pre-decimal coinage, 21 shillings, or one pound one shilling.

gum, *n.* a light glue, used for paper mostly.

gun, *n.* sometimes this means a place in a game-shooting group. Advertisements in country-life magazines sometimes begin "Fourth gun wanted . . ."

gunsmith, *n.* a manufacturer of guns.

Guy Fawkes Night, *prop. n.* November 5th, celebrated with bonfires and fireworks, to mark the foiling of a plot to blow up the Houses of Parliament led by Guy Fawkes in 1605. A **guy** is an effigy of Guy Fawkes, traditionally burned on a bonfire on the night.

haberdasher, *n.* a seller of notions and small items connected with clothes, such as buttons. He does *not* sell clothes.

hack, *v.* to kick someone deliberately in a game.

hacking jacket, *n.* a riding jacket, with tight waist, slanted pockets with flaps and vents, or a sports jacket that follows this style.

haggis, *n.* a Scottish national dish eaten by no one but Scots, consisting of sheep's entrails with oats and other things added, sewn up in the lining of a sheep's stomach. To an Englishman an object of awe, distaste, and lurid speculation.

ha-ha, *n.* a sunken wall or fence dividing a field, usually a landscaped garden, from the surrounding countryside, so constructed as to give an unimpaired view.

hake, *n.* an edible fish, related to the cod.

half dollar, *n.* (colloq.) 12½ pence or, in the old terminology, a half-crown. (See **dollar**.)

half-inch, *v.* (colloq.) to steal, Cockney rhyming slang ("pinch").

hall of residence, *n.* a dormitory building for students. A "dormitory" in British is always one room where a number of people sleep.

Harley Street, *prop. n.* the area in London where the highest-rated doctors practice.

hat-trick, *n.* a cricket term, it means bowling out (an approximate equivalent of striking out) three batsmen (batters) in a row. It is also used outside cricket to mean any string of three successes.

headmaster or **head,** *n.* the principal of a school.

Heath Robinson, *n.* any device of comic complexity. This is the name of a popular cartoonist who specialized in drawing these.

Heinz, *n.* at the racetrack, 57 bets in combination (from the old Heinz 57 varieties) involving six horses.

helter skelter, *n.* a spiral slide at a fairground.

High Church, *prop. n.* and *adj.* a Church of England style close to Roman Catholicism, with an emphasis on ritual and the liturgy. Sometimes called Anglo-Catholic.

High Street or **the high street,** *n.* Main Street, the principal shopping street of a small town.

high tea, *n.* a late afternoon meal, replacing tea (see **tea**) and supper, usually containing some elements of each.

hire, *v.* to rent something from someone. In Britain, you hire a car or a radio or television set. However, one rents a dwelling place.

hire purchase, *n.* installment plan.

hive off, *v.* to separate from the main body, e.g., "They're hiving off the overseas operation and making it a separate company."

hoarding, *n.* billboard.

hob, *n.* the top of a stove, on which things are cooked.

Hobson's choice, *n.* something presented as a choice, but in which one has no real alternative. As it was explained in 1700,

> Where to elect there is but one,
> 'Tis Hobson's choice, Take that or none.
> —from *England Reformed* by Thomas Ward.

hockey, *n.* field hockey.

hogmanay, *n.* the Scottish New Year's Eve, traditionally celebrated with much drink and festivity (New Year's Day is a public holiday in Scotland, not in England and Wales) and many old traditions. Evelyn Waugh, in *Decline and Fall,* defined it deflatingly as "being sick on Glasgow pavements."

hokey cokey, *n.* a kind of urban folk dance.

holdall, *n.* a soft suitcase, a tote bag.

Home Counties, *prop. n.* the counties that border on London, containing much of exurbia. Often used as a synonym for smart exurbia and its life style.

Home Office, *prop. n.* the Government department responsible for law and order and other domestic affairs, including immigration. **Home Secretary,** *prop. n.* the minister in charge of this department, a senior member of the cabinet.

homely, *adj.* home-loving, running a good home. Used about someone's appearance, it can mean pleasant and comfortable, and is not necessarily insulting.

honorary, *adj.* unpaid. The Hon. Secretary or Hon. Treasurer of an organization is unpaid and doing it in his spare time.

Honourable, *adj.* an honorific applied (but not in speaking to them) to the younger son of an earl and to all the children of a viscount or baron. The term is not applied to Members of Parliament, though when referring to one another in the House, members must use it, e.g., "The Honourable member for Bexley." The term "Right Honourable" is applied to members of the **Privy Council.**

honours list, *n.* the roll of those people who receive new titles of nobility and other honors. There are two of these each year, "New Year Honours," announced on January 1st, and the "Birthday Honours," on the day in June designated as the Queen's official birthday, which changes from year to year.

hood, *n.* the soft top of a converti-ble. A car's hood is a bonnet in British.

hoot, *n.* something funny. "It's a hoot!" means "It's a riot!"

hoover, *n.* and *v.* a vacuum cleaner. The brand name has come to signify the appliance itself. It is used as a verb, to hoover.

hounds, *n.* in the singular this could conceivably mean any kind of dog, but in the plural it means only fox hounds, and is used in connection with fox hunting.

houseman, *n.* an intern in a hospital.

housey housey, *n.* a form of bingo, traditional in the services.

housing development or **housing estate,** *n.* housing project.

hump, *v.* to carry something heavy.

hump, *n.* (colloq.) a fit of bad temper or annoyance, as in "He's got the hump."

hundredweight, *n.* 112 pounds, perversely, instead of the American hundredweight's 100 pounds.

hunt, *v.* fox hunting, unless otherwise specified.

hustings, *n.* electionary meetings. There is no singular for this. Going on the stump is going on the hustings.

ice, *n.* ice cream. Both terms are used. "Ice" also means ice.

Identikit, *n.* the composition of a

pictorial likeness of someone by putting together a number of facial characteristics by a particular method. It was devised by Hugh C. MacDonald of Los Angeles, but is now used mostly by the British police.

industrial, *adj.* often referring to labor, as in "industrial dispute" and "industrial reporter."

infant school, *n.* the first two years of school, covering ages 5–6.

Inland Revenue, *n.* Internal Revenue.

inquiry agent, *n.* private detective.

instructor, *n.* a teacher in a technical or vocational institution, not a college or university.

ironmongery, *n.* hardware. An **ironmonger's** is a hardware store.

jar, *n.* (colloq.) a drink in a pub. Mostly Irish and Northern.

jelly, *n.* Jell-O.

jemmy, *n.* jimmy.

joiner, *n.* a carpenter who does small, often delicate, domestic work.

joinery, *n.* woodwork.

joint, *n.* a piece of meat for roasting.

judge's rules, *n.* the rules governing the treatment of an arrested person by the police.

judy, *n.* girl. Working-class.

jumble sale, *n.* rummage sale.

jumper, *n.* a light pullover.

junction, *n.* intersection of roads.

junior school, *n.* the second phase of school, covering ages 7–11.

kedgeree, *n.* a dish made of rice and shredded fish.

kerfuffle, *n.* (colloq.) a row or disturbance.

kettle, *n.* teakettle. Any other kind is a pot or casserole in Britain. The one culinary exception is a **fish kettle,** a long narrow utensil for boiling fish. Hence the expression, when something is fouled up, "That's a fine kettle of fish!"

khyber, *n.* (colloq.) fanny. Rhyming slang: Khyber Pass—arse (they rhyme if you pronounce "pass" as the British do).

kinky, *adj.* sexually odd or quirky. This has now almost swamped any other meaning.

kip, *n.* (colloq.) a short sleep, a nap.

kipper, *n.* kippered (dried and smoked) herring, a popular breakfast food.

knacker, *n.* a horse slaughterer. **knacker's yard,** *n.* the place where horses are slaughtered.

knickers, *n.* old-fashioned women's underpants, like bloomers.

knighthood, *n.* one of several honors bestowed for services to the nation. They all carry the title Sir, and none is hereditary. The wife of a knight is Lady ——.

knock off, *v.* (colloq.) steal.

knock up, *v.* 1. to look up someone or wake up someone. Many an American man has been startled by an invitation from an Englishwoman to "Knock me up some time." It doesn't mean that. 2. To make or fabricate something quickly, like a meal or a homemade piece of furniture.

labourer, *n.* an unskilled outdoor workman, on a farm or construction site.

Labour Exchange, *n.* the old-fashioned name for the government-run office which tries to find jobs for unemployed people, more commonly used than the officially correct name, **Employment Exchange.**

Labour Party, *prop. n.* one of the two main political parties in Britain, it covers a wide spectrum of opinion from the center leftward. It was founded in 1900 as the Labour Representation Committee to give labor unions a voice in Parliament, and the unions are still corporate members, but it is an independent party and far from being simply the voice of organized labor.

ladder, *n.* a run in hose or stockings.

Lady, *n.* a form of address which usually prefixes the name of a countess, marchioness, viscountess, or baroness, the wife of a baronet or knight, and the daughter of a duke, marquess, or an earl. In the last-named cases, the title precedes the first name, e.g., Lady Jane Bigglesworth.

ladybird, *n.* ladybug.

lag, *n.* (colloq.) a long-time occupant of prisons.

lager, *n.* a light beer, with a more sophisticated appeal than the more widely consumed **bitter.**

lame duck, *n.* an ailing business or other venture. The American political meaning is unknown in Britain.

lamp-post, *n.* streetlamp.

Lancashire hot pot, *n.* a meat-and-potato stew.

lance corporal, *n.* the first army rank above a buck private.

lashings, *n.* large servings of food or drink, e.g., "roast beef with lashings of Yorkshire pudding and gravy."

lavatory, *n.* toilet.

lay, *v.* the table—to set the table.

layabout, *n.* a loafer, someone who does not work.

lay-by, *n.* a pull-off on a freeway.

lay on, *v.* to organize, arrange. A tourist guide might tell a party that "lunch and a visit to the castle are laid on for today."

leader or **leading article,** *n.* an editorial in a newspaper.

left luggage office, *n.* checkroom.

legal aid, *n.* payment from government funds for legal services for someone who cannot afford it himself, a feature of Britain's welfare system.

level crossing, *n.* railroad crossing.

Liberal Jew, *prop. n.* a Jew roughly similar to a Reform Jew in America in the degree of his deviation from orthodoxy. Jewish religious practice in Britain is divided into three streams, from right to left: orthodox, reform and liberal.

Liberal Party, *prop. n.* a small political party, third party in a two-party system, with very few Members of Parliament. It was one of the two major parties for nearly a century, until it was finally replaced by the Labour Party as the party of the liberal left in the 1920s.

liberty, *n.* cheek, impudence. "Don't take liberties with me" means "Don't get fresh with me." "He's got a liberty!" means "He's got a nerve!"

licensee, *n.* the manager of a pub, the person who holds the license to run it.

licensing laws, *n.* the laws governing when and where liquor may be sold. Excise laws cover only taxation and import.

lie-in, *n.* a rest in bed in the morning.

life peer, *n.* someone who has been given the title of baron or baroness and accompanying seat in the House of Lords, which are for life only and are not passed on to his descendants. This new form of nobleman was created by an act of Parliament in 1958.

lift, *n.* elevator.

light ale, *n.* pale ale, usually slightly sweeter than other light beers.

limited or **Ltd.,** *adj.* incorporated. It stands for "limited liability."

lineage, *n.* on newspapers, payment by space.

line shoot, *n.* (colloq.) a boastful tale; to "shoot a line" is to exaggerate or fabricate one's exploits or position. World War II R.A.F. slang.

lip-balm, *n.* Chap-stick. One American visitor says that when he asked his hotel porter in London where he could get a Chapstick, he was directed to a Chinese restaurant.

living, *n.* in the Church of England, the tenure of office of a parson resulting from a donation.

loaf, *n.* (colloq.) head, brains. It is Cockney rhyming slang: loaf of bread—head.

lobby correspondent, *n.* the political correspondent of a newspaper, so called because he is a member of the small group of journalists who are allowed into the members' lobby of the House of Commons.

local, *n.* (colloq.) the particular pub that is an Englishman's meeting place, and sometimes home away from home. He might say, "The Volunteer Arms is my local; which one do you use?"

locum, *n.* a doctor or lawyer substituting for another during a temporary absence.

lodger, *n.* roomer.

logic chopping, *v.* academic hair-splitting.

lollipop man, *n.* a man who escorts children across the road outside a school, so called because he carries a pole with a large circular sign on the end, shaped like a lollipop.

lolly, *n.* (colloq.) money.

long jump, *n.* broad jump.

loo, *n.* (colloq.) toilet. A genteel colloquialism, this.

loofah, *n.* a bath sponge, called this because it is made from a loofah plant.

long vac, *n.* the universities' three-month summer vacation.

Lord, *prop. n.* a form of address to any nobleman below a duke. One never speaks in Britain of "a lord."

Lord Chancellor, *prop. n.* the head of the judiciary, who is ex officio speaker of the House of Lords and a member of the cabinet.

Lord Lieutenant, *n.* an office-holder, usually a nobleman who in theory holds powers in an area deputed by the monarch, but whose functions in fact are largely ceremonial. Pronounced "Lord Leftenant."

Lord Privy Seal, *prop. n.* an office, with duties that are now obsolete, retained so as to give some leading politician a title that carries with it a position in the cabinet, as a kind of Minister Without Portfolio.

Lords, *prop. n.* Britain's principal cricket stadium, in London.

Lords, *n.* the House of Lords, the upper house of Parliament, though much less important politically than the House of Commons. It consists of most peers (barons and upward) and the leaders of the Church of England.

lorry, *n.* truck.

loud hailer, *n.* megaphone.

Low Church, *prop. n.* a Church of England style that is very Protestant, emphasizing simplicity and direct participation in the service.

L-plate, *n.* "L" sign on a car signifying that the driver is still learning. Required by law.

lucky dip, *n.* grab bag.

Ludo, *n.* a common children's game with board, dice, and counters.

lug-hole, *n.* (colloq.) ear.

lumber, *v.* to make someone do a job or handle the situation, e.g., "Everyone else was going on holiday so they lumbered me with it." Very much used in the reflexive: there was a popular song called "I've Been Lumbered."

lumber room, *n.* a spare room where things are stored.

lump, *n.* casual, nonunion building workers. They have been dubbed, collectively, "the lump" by regular workers in the trade; the word comes from "lumpenproletariat."

lump, *v.* (colloq.) to accept unwillingly, but without much choice. "Like it or lump it" is a common saying.

luncheon voucher, *n.* a voucher given by some employers to staff in addition to salary which can be exchanged for food in a restaurant.

mackintosh, *n.* raincoat. The word is becoming less common. Often shortened to mac.

maisonette, *n.* a duplex apartment, often part of a house.

managing director, *n.* the chief executive officer of a corporation.

Mancunian, *prop. n.* a citizen of Manchester.

manse, *n.* the home of a minister of the Church of Scotland, a term redolent of frugality, asceticism, and high principles.

Manx, *prop. adj.* pertaining to the Isle of Man, a small island off northwest England. A **Manx cat** is a breed of tail-less cat.

market garden, *n.* truck farm.

marriage lines, *n.* marriage certificate.

marrow, *n.* a native vegetable, a kind of a large squash.

martini, *n.* a popular brand of vermouth, often drunk straight as an aperitif. If you ask simply for a "martini" at most British pubs, you are likely to be given a glass of vermouth rather than a cocktail. Even prefixing it with "dry" may get you only a dry vermouth. A request for a "martini cocktail" might get you there.

mason, *n.* a worker in stone, never, as in America, in brick as well.

mate, *n.* friend, pal. Working-class.

maths, *n.* math.

Mayfair, *prop. n.* the smart, rich district in the center of London.

mayor, *n.* the chairman of a municipal or borough council, whose activities outside the council chamber are ceremonial. He does not have the executive power of an American mayor, nor is he elected directly.

may tree, *n.* a hawthorn tree (but the British use "hawthorn bush").

M.B.E., *n.* Medal of the British Empire, awarded for service to the nation.

mean, *adj.* stingy, tight with money. It does not usually mean nasty in the more general sense.

Meccano, *prop. n.* the most popular boys' construction set, similar to an Erector set.

mental, *adj.* (colloq.) mentally ill, insane.

merchant bank, *n.* investment bank.

mess kit, *n.* formal military dress for dining in the officers' mess.

Messrs., *prop. pron.* an abbreviation of Messieurs, a formal mode of address often used in business correspondence to a firm, e.g., "Messrs. Bloggs, Blunt and Bottomley, solicitors . . ."

methylated spirits, *n*. similar to wood alcohol. **meths drinker,** *n*. an alcoholic bum reduced to drinking this.

Metropolitan Police, *prop. n.* the London police.

mews, *n*. an alley, often a very fashionable one, that used to contain stables with living space for the grooms and other staff above, and now consists of town houses or apartments, sometimes with garages where the stables were. There is at least one mews in New York City, Washington Mews near Washington Square.

M.F.H., *n*. master of fox hounds, the man who directs a regular fox hunt and sets its standards, a position of some social standing.

M.I.5, *prop. n.* the domestic intelligence, or counterespionage service. The initials stood originally for Military Intelligence.

M.I.6, *prop. n.* the intelligence service that operates overseas, roughly equivalent to the C.I.A. Strictly speaking, the terms M.I.5 and M.I.6 are obsolete; the names were changed a few years ago, and both were incorporated into the Special Intelligence Services, or S.I.S. But outside the intelligence community, the M.I. terms are still used generally. The government won't correct anyone since it will rarely admit that any such organizations exist.

mick, *n*. (colloq.) an Irishman. A neutral term, quite acceptable to Irishmen.

mickey, *n*. (colloq.) to "take the mickey out of" someone means to make fun of him.

Midlands, *n*. central England.

mild, *n*. mild ale, a dark-colored ale with less hop flavoring than light ale. **Mild and bitter** used to be a favorite drink, but as pubs change, it is seen less.

milk float, *n*. a small dairy delivery truck.

Mills bomb, *n*. a World War I hand grenade. Rep. Wilbur Mills' protectionist trade bill was called by British exporters "the Mills bomb."

minced meat or **mince,** *n*. hamburger meat.

mineral water, *n*. any carbonated soft drink.

mingy, *adj*. meager, scanty.

mini-cab, *n*. a car that serves as a taxi in answer to calls, but is not licensed to cruise for fares.

minim, *n*. a half note. Musical.

mistress, *n*. a member of the teaching staff in a girls' school. When, during World War II, the R.A.F. took over a famous girls' boarding school called Roedean to billet trainee pilots, the new arrivals found next to every bed a button and a notice saying: "If you want a mistress during the night, ring this bell." The first night was bedlam, so the story goes.

mix, *v.* (colloq.) to cause dissension, such as by spreading false tales. A **mixer** is someone who makes trouble in this way. To **mix it** sometimes means to row or fight.

mixed grill, *n.* a dish of several kinds of grilled meat with mushrooms and tomatoes.

mob, *n.* (colloq.) apart from its literal meaning of an angry crowd, this means a group of people in a much less pejorative sense than in American. "Our mob" means something like "our gang," and a man will speak of his outfit in the army as his mob.

moleskin, *n.* a rough cotton fabric.

monkey, *n.* (colloq.) £500.

monochrome, *n.* black and white TV film.

moonlight flit, *n.* (colloq.) a departure by night to avoid paying rent that is owed.

moonshine, *n.* (colloq.) poppycock, nonsense.

moor, *n.* an area of flat, rough, open country.

moped, *n.* a mini-bike, a low-powered motorcycle.

morning room, *n.* dinette.

Moss Bros., *n.* not the author's two sons, but a London firm which hires out clothes, particularly evening dress. The name has become another term for hired finery—e.g., "You're wearing your Moss Bros. tonight, I see" —and the subject of innumerable jokes. Usually pronounced "Moss Bross."

M.O.T., *prop. n.* Ministry of Transport. Used about a car, it means that it has passed the Ministry's roadworthiness test.

motorist, *n.* car driver. A newspaper's **motoring correspondent** covers the automobile industry.

motorway, *n.* a superhighway. The big motorways in Britain are called M-1, M-2, and so on.

mouth organ, *n.* harmonica.

M.P., *n.* Member of Parliament; actually, of the House of Commons, the elected house. The letters are put after a member's name, e.g., John Smith, M.P.

Mr., *prop. n.* as well as an ordinary form of address, this is also given to a dentist or a doctor who has attained the rank of surgeon. Americans going for medical treatment in Britain have sometimes drawn back when they found the practitioner described as "Mr. So-and-so," and said they wanted to see a qualified doctor. In fact, he is a doctor of elevated status.

Mrs. Mop, *prop. n.* (colloq.) a cleaning lady.

muck about, *v.* (colloq.) to mess about.

mucker, *n.* (colloq.) friend. Very working-class.

muck in, *v.* (colloq.) to pitch in together.

mufti, *adj.* civilian clothes, as distinct from a uniform.

mug, *n.* sucker. **mug's game,** *n.* (colloq.) something which cannot be profitable.

muggins, *n.* (colloq.) a sucker. Usually used without the article, e.g., "I was muggins."

mum, *n.* (colloq.) mom, ma.

music hall, *n.* vaudeville.

muslin, *n.* cheesecloth.

mustard pickle, *n.* cucumbers pickled in mustard sauce.

NAAFI, *prop. n.* a canteen for servicemen; the British PX. An acronym of Navy, Army, and Air Force Institute.

nancy or **nancy boy,** *n.* homosexual.

nap, *n.* a strong tip—to "go nap" on something means to stake a lot on it.

nappy, *n.* diaper.

nark, *n.* (colloq.) an informer.

National Assistance, *prop. n.* the system of welfare payments to the needy. The official name has been changed now; the payments are "supplementary benefits" and the office is the Social Security office, but the old term is still much used.

National Insurance, *prop. n.* the scheme of compulsory government insurance, part of the premium being paid by the employee and part by his employer.

national service, *n.* peacetime military conscription, abolished in Britain in 1958; service as a peacetime conscript, e.g., "I was doing my national service."

naturalisation papers, *n.* citizenship papers.

navvy, *n.* an unskilled workman on roadwork. The word originated in the first part of the nineteenth century, when it was applied to the men who dug the navigational canals that crisscrossed Britain.

nearside, *adj.* in driving, this refers to the side of the car nearer the edge of the road. In Britain this is the left side, in America the right.

neat, *adj.* straight, of a drink, e.g., neat whisky is straight whisky.

needle, *n.* (colloq.) ill-will or a grudge, e.g., "He's got the needle" or "That gives me the needle."

never-never, *n.* (colloq.) installment plan.

new town, *n.* a town built up from scratch as government policy, near London or another urban center to take the overspill.

nib, *n.* a pen point, other than a ball-point.

nick, *v.* (colloq.) to steal.

nick, *n.* (colloq.) 1. prison. 2. condition of an article, e.g., "A ten-year-old car but it's in good nick."

nicker, *n.* (colloq.) a pound sterling. The plural form is the same, e.g., "ten nicker."

night club, *n.* a night spot to which only members can go. Many of these, like strip clubs, are clubs in name only to comply with aspects of the law, and anyone coming off the street can become a member and go in.

nightdress, *n.* nightgown.

nip, *n,* a shot of liquor.

nip, *v.* to go briefly, e.g., "I'll just nip down to the corner."

nipper, *n.* (colloq.) child, kid.

Nissen hut, *n.* Quonset hut.

nit, *n.* a fool.

nob, *n.* (colloq.) a big shot, someone of social standing. Most British visitors to San Francisco assume that it is an American word that gave Nob Hill its name.

nobble, *v.* (colloq.) to get at and influence or persuade, e.g., "He tried to nobble some members of the inquiry board." In racing, it means to dope or injure a horse.

noggin, *n.* (colloq.) a drink of beer or spirits.

Nonconformist, *prop. adj.* a Protestant church in Britain that is not in communion with the Church of England, such as Baptist or Presbyterian.

Norfolk Broads, *prop. n.* not the local girls, but a low-lying area of Norfolk with interconnected stretches of water, popular for boating vacations. Often called just the Broads.

Norman, *prop. adj.* pertaining to the period after the Norman Conquest of England in 1066.

nosh, nosh up, *n.* (colloq.) a new and voguish word in Britain, it means food and, in particular, a slap-up meal. It has changed meaning in coming over from Yiddish-American, where nosh means a bite or snack.

note, *n.* a Treasury bill. One speaks of a pound note, not bill.

notepaper, *n.* writing paper. A genteel term for it.

nous, *n.* (colloq.) rhyming with "mouse," savvy, intelligence in a particular situation, e.g., "He didn't have the political nous to take advantage of it."

number plate, *n.* a license plate on a car.

nursing home, *n.* a private hospital.

nut, *n.* of butter, a knob of butter.

oast house, *n.* a building containing a kiln for drying the hops or malt used in making beer. It has a roof in the shape of a sloping cone, a feature of the countryside in some parts of England.

O.B.E., *prop. n.* the Order of the British Empire, awarded for many kinds of service to the nation. The letters, as the initials of other decorations or orders of chivalry, are put after a person's name.

OCTU, *prop. n.* Officer Cadet Training School.

odds-on, *n.* and *adj.* better than even odds. A horse running at 5–6 is the odds-on favorite.

off-license, *n.* a liquor store. The term comes from its license to sell liquor for consumption off the premises.

offside, *adj.* in driving, the side of the car away from the sidewalk. (See **nearside.**)

off-the-peg, *adj.* ready-made, of clothes.

oilskins, *n.* oilers.

Old Bailey, *n.* the principal London criminal court.

old boy, *n.* an old grad, or alumnus. A school has an old boys' reunion, not an alumni reunion. Similarly, **old girls** are alumnae.

old boy network, *n.* the supposed system by which people of the same upper-class school background extend mutual help in getting ahead.

Old Contemptibles, *prop. n.* veterans of the British Army that went to France in 1914 in the early months of World War I, or often, more loosely, of the World War I army. The term comes from a remark of the Kaiser, who termed the 1914 British Expeditionary Force a "contemptible little army," an opinion he was soon to change. Characteristically, the British soldiers took this up as a sobriquet, and bore it proudly.

O-levels, *n.* a series of important exams taken at age 15 or 16.

O.M., *prop. n.* Order of Merit. An award given by the nation for exceptional life-long achievement. Members of the order are limited to 24, plus an occasional foreign member. The last American member was General Eisenhower.

on-camera, *n.* in television, a stand-up piece.

one-over-the-eight, *adj.* drunk.

o.n.o., *n.* or nearest offer. Seen often in ads, e.g., "For sale, £150 o.n.o. . . ."

open-cast mining, *n.* strip mining.

opening time, *n.* the time set by law as which pubs may open and sell drinks, usually 11:30 in the morning and five o'clock in the afternoon, varying slightly by districts.

operating theatre, *n.* operating room in a hospital.

oppo, *n.* (colloq.) close companion. Working-class.

Ordnance Survey, *prop. n.* the official maps of Britain produced by the Government.

ostler, *n.* hostler.

other ranks, *n.* servicemen (or women) other than commissioned officers.

outfitter's or **men's outfitter's,** *n.* haberdasher's.

outsize, *adj.* extra-large, of clothes. A term much used by stores, to break it to the customer gently.

Oxbridge, *prop. n.* a compound of the names of Britain's two senior universities, Oxford and Cambridge, used about them jointly, e.g., "Oxbridge graduates no longer predominate among diplomatic service entrants. . . ."—from a report in *The Times* of London.

Oxonian, *prop. adj.* pertaining to Oxford University.

paddle-steamer, *n.* a sidewheeler.

paddy, *n.* (colloq.) 1. an Irishman, usually an Irish workman. 2. a state of high emotion or excitement. "Don't get in such a paddy!" means "Cool down."

paddy waggon, *n.* Black Maria.

palais, *n.* a dance hall. They are often called Palais de Danse, pronounced the French way.

pale ale, *n.* light ale, light in color and body.

palm court, *n.* a hotel lounge decorated with potted palms. Popular in the '20s and '30s, the phrase is often used to denote that kind of atmosphere; palm court music is the kind of soupy, romantic, string music played by a palm court orchestra.

panda car, *n.* police patrol car.

panel, *n.* a doctor's list of National Health Service patients.

pantechnicon, *n.* a furniture-removal truck.

pantomime, *n.* a traditional stylized Christmas entertainment for children. It is based loosely on one of the well-known nursery stories, and its special features are songs, spectacle, a hero played by a girl (the "principal boy") and a comic old woman played by a man (the "dame"). Sometimes shortened to **panto.**

pants, *n.* underpants. Pants are trousers in Britain.

paraffin, *n.* kerosene.

parish, *n.* a civil administrative district, which usually follows the boundaries of the ecclesiastical district.

parish pump, *n.* and *adj.* parochial, village-minded, referring to the gossip of women around the pump where they used to get their water, e.g., "parish pump politics."

parky, *adj.* (colloq.) sharp, biting, referring to the weather.

pasty or **patty,** *n.* a small meat pie.

patience, *n.* the game of solitaire.

pavement, *n.* sidewalk.

P.A.Y.E., *prop. n.* pay as you earn, the system of taxation in which the tax is deducted from wages at source.

p.b.i., *n.* (colloq.) infantry. It stands for "poor bloody infantry."

P.C., *prop. n.* Police Constable. A policeman on the beat is identified as P.C.—followed by his name or number.

Pearly King/Queen, *n.* a leader in a community of pushcart peddlers who, in accordance with tradition, covers his/her clothes with mother-of-pearl buttons.

pease pudding, *n.* a pudding made with peas, usually served with ham or bacon.

peckish, *adj.* (colloq.) slightly hungry.

peer, *n.* someone of noble rank.

peppercorn rent, *n.* a purely nominal rent. It dates from the day when the nominal rent paid to a feudal lord was one pepper-corn per year.

perks, *n.* fringe benefits. Short for perquisites.

petrol, *n.* gasoline.

petty sessions, *n.* a court in which a magistrate hears minor cases.

pi, *adj.* (colloq.) virtuous, pious. Upper-class.

pick-axe, *n.* pick.

pick-me-up, *n.* pick-up, in the sense of a reviver.

pillar box, *n.* standard mailbox for mailing letters, red and cylindrical.

pinafore, *n.* a woman's apron.

pinch, *v.* (colloq.) 1. steal: a light-weight word, like "swipe." At Christmas, 1937, which followed shortly on the abdication and marriage of King Edward VIII, schoolchildren in England adapted the carol to:

Hark the herald angels sing.
Mrs. Simpson's pinched our king.
2. arrest.

pint, *n.* 1. slightly larger than a pint in America, 34.68 cubic inches, against an American (liquid) pint's 28.87 cubic inches. 2. used by itself, collo-quially, it means a pint of beer, the standard large-sized glass served in pubs, as in "Let's go and have a pint."

pip, *v.* to beat by a very small margin, e.g., "The favorite was pipped at the post."

pip, *n.* "It gives me the pip"

means it annoys me, makes me angry.

pissed, *adj.* (colloq.) drunk.

pissed-off, *adj.* (colloq.) fed-up, irritated.

piss off! *v.* (colloq.) scram! an offensive phrase.

pitch, *n.* the ground on which soccer or cricket is played.

place, *n.* at the racetrack, coming in second or third, not just second, as at American tracks.

plaice, *n.* a flat North Sea fish, often eaten fried.

platelayer, *n.* track layer on the railroad.

play up, *v.* make fun of.

plimsolls, *n.* sneakers.

plonk, *n.* (colloq.) cheap wine. A genial term, which does not insult the drink.

plough, *v.* to fail in exams, at university. The verb is transitive: an examiner ploughs a student, a student is ploughed.

P.M., *abbr.* Prime Minister.

po, *n.* chamber pot. This word is dropping out of use.

po-faced, *adj.* (colloq.) with an uptight face, solemn and expressionless.

point, *n.* 1. an electrical outlet. Also **power point.** 2. on the railroad, a switch.

point duty, *n.* a policeman's traffic duty.

poke, *v.* (colloq.) to fornicate with, brusquely.

polka dots, *n.* chocolate chips. They would know this in a food store in Britain, but it is not widely used. Nobody would understand "chocolate chips."

polytechnic, *n.* an institute of higher education that does not have the status of a university or, normally, any resident students.

ponce, *n.* and *v.* pimp.

pong, *n.* and *v.* (colloq.) smell, odor, e.g., "After a few months it began to pong a bit."

pontoon, *n.* another name for the card game blackjack, or twenty-one.

pony, *n.* (colloq) . £25.

pools, *n.* short for football pools, a weekly contest to predict the results of the Saturday soccer matches, in which there are big money prizes. Some five million people fill in pools coupons regularly.

pop, *v.* to go, or put, with small effort, e.g., "I'll just pop next door," or "Pop it in the oven a half-hour before dinnertime."

poppet, *n.* honey, sweetie. A term of endearment. Mostly a woman's word.

porridge, *n.* oatmeal.

porter, *n.* a doorman. In a market, someone who carries produce. It also has the American meaning of someone who carries bags.

posh, *adj.* ultra-smart, high-toned. Though this word has crossed the Atlantic, it is worth including here, first because it is still much more British than American, and second because *Webster's Dictionary* says its origin is unknown. Actually, it dates back to the heyday of Britain's eastern empire, and is an acronym of "port out, starboard home." On the ships taking Britain's imperial officials and their families to the Far East, the most sought-after and most expensive cabins were on the port side of the ship on the way out and the starboard side on the way home, because these were the ones most shielded from the strong sun.

post, *n.* and *v.* mail. Also **postman, post bag,** etc. "Mail" is used often for mail that travels long distances, so that one has air mail and a mail train.

poste restante, *n.* to be held at the post office for collection.

posting, *n.* an assignment somewhere for a considerable duration. In the foreign service and the services, for instance, they speak of a posting abroad, or of being posted.

potman, *n.* the man who collects the glasses and cleans up in a pub.

potty, *adj.* (colloq.) crazy.

pouf, pouffe, *n.* 1. a stuffed stool, a hassock. 2. (colloq.) a homosexual.

pourer, *n.* a spout attached to a bottle.

power point, see **point.**

pram, *n.* baby carriage.

prang, *v.* and *n.* (colloq.) to crash or damage in an accident; a crash. R.A.F. slang.

prefect, *n.* a monitor, a pupil chosen to help enforce school discipline.

preggers, *adj.* pregnant.

preliminary hearing, *n.* a hearing before a magistrate to decide whether there is a case to answer. Similar to a grand jury hearing, only there is no jury.

premium bond, *n.* a government bond for one pound sterling that carries no interest, but instead a chance to win a big-money prize in a lottery.

prep, *n.* homework. Upper-class.

prep school, *n.* a private school with the social status of a public school (British) but taking boys or girls at pre-public-school age, that is, up to 13.

press gang, *n.* two centuries ago, this was the group of sailors who used to force men into the navy. Now the term is used as a verb and metaphorically; someone may say he was "press ganged into" doing something.

primary school, *n.* grade school, up to the age of 11.

primus stove, *n.* a portable kerosene stove.

principal boy, *n.* one of the stars of a **pantomime** (see), a girl playing a young man.

Privy Council, *prop. n.* the group of ministers, former ministers, and others who traditionally advised the monarch. As a group they still have some constitutional functions.

Privy purse, *n.* the money voted by Parliament for the personal expenses of the monarch.

probe, *n.* a dental explorer, the sharp implement with which a dentist explores someone's teeth for cavities.

producer, *n.* in the theater, the man who directs the play. The man listed as the producer on a playbill in Britain would be called the director in an American one. However, in the movies, the American terminology is followed, and in the theater also "director" is sometimes used now as it would be in America.

professor, *n.* the chairman of a department at a university. There is only one professor to a department, so the title is a rarer distinction in Britain than in America.

prom concert or **proms,** *n.* a concert at which most of the audience stand in the concert hall.

provinces, *n.* all of Britain outside London, e.g., "The play had an eight-week tour in the provinces before coming to London."

provost, *n.* the mayor of a Scottish city. (See **mayor.**)

publican, *n.* the manager of a pub, rather than the kind of tax collector coupled with sinners in the New Testament.

public bar, *n.* one of the two or three bars in most pubs, the cheaper by a very small amount.

public school, *n.* a private school, usually a boarding school, which takes boys or girls (almost none is coeducational) from the age of about 13 up to university age. These have a social as well as an educational status.

pukka, *adj.* genuine, sound. An Anglo-Indian word, usually used in an imperial atmosphere, or else for comic effect.

punchball, *n.* a punching bag.

punch-up, *n.* (colloq.) a fight.

punter, *n.* someone who bets.

purchase tax, *n.* a kind of sales tax levied directly on a store and passed on to the buyer. Now replaced by **V.A.T.** (see).

put down, *v.* used about an animal, it means to have it killed painlessly.

quack, *n.* (colloq.) doctor. The term implies no denigration of the doctor to whom it is applied; it seems to stem from a defensive philistinism.

quantity surveyor, *n.* a person who estimates the amount of materials required for a building.

quart, *n.* 69.35 cubic inches, against the American (liquid) quart's 57.75 cubic inches.

quaver, *n.* eighth note. Musical.

Queen Anne, *prop. n.* the architectural style of the early eighteenth century, when Queen Anne was on the throne, characterized by classical simplicity of line and detail.

Queen's Counsel, *prop. n.* an honorary rank for a barrister, signified by the letters Q.C. after his name. Becoming a Q.C. is known as "taking silk." When a king is on the throne, the Q.C. becomes a K.C.

queer, *adj.* in addition to its colloquial meaning of homosexual, in which sense it is used mostly by young people, this can also mean "unwell." Soon after arriving in England after an American upbringing, I was told one day, in a friendly tone, "You're looking a bit queer today, lad." I said apologetically, "Oh, really? Perhaps it's this suit."

queue, *n.* and *v.* a line of people waiting, or, as a verb, to wait in line. A Dutchman of my acquaintance, arriving at London airport, was waiting at a pay station to make a call and was baffled when someone asked him, in all seriousness, "Are you the queue?" When this was interpreted and they decided between them that he was, the man fell into place behind him to wait his turn.

quid, *n.* (colloq.) a pound sterling.

rabbit, *v.* (colloq.) to talk, chat. Cockney rhyming slang (rabbit-and-pork—talk).

racecourse, *n.* racetrack.

Rachmanism, *n.* slum-landlord practices. The word comes from the name of a notorious slum landlord who received a great deal of publicity at one point because he was a member of the Christine Keeler–Mandy Rice-Davies circle.

RADA, *prop. n.* the Royal Academy of Dramatic Art, the leading British drama school.

rag, *n.* student revelries, characterized by boisterousness and stunts. At some colleges and universities, this is formalized in a "rag week."

rag, *v.* to tease, josh.

rag and bone man, *n.* junkman.

railway, *n.* railroad.

ramp, *n.* a swindle, or a falsehood spread to make someone a profit.

rates, *n.* local property taxes.

rating, *n.* an enlisted man in the Royal Navy.

Rawlplug, *n.* a small plug inserted in a wall as a fixing for a screw, similar to a Mollybolt. A trade name now used widely.

reader, *n.* a kind of assistant professor.

reception centre, *n.* a center established by the local authorities for homeless families.

recorder, *n.* a judge in a lower court.

redbrick, *adj.* referring to the older universities other than Oxford, Cambridge, and London.

redcap, *n.* military policeman.

reef knot, *n.* a square knot.

reel, *n.* a spool of cotton, wire, tape, etc.

Reform Jew, *prop. n.* roughly similar to a Conservative Jew in America.

Regency, *n.* and *adj.* the style or fashion of the period 1810–1820, when the future George IV was Prince Regent. "Architecturally, some of Brighton's streets are still Regency streets"—a tourist board guide.

reggae, *n.* West Indian rock music brought to Britain by Caribbean immigrants.

registrar, *n.* a senior doctor in a hospital, ranking just below a consultant.

reserve price, *n.* a set price at an auction below which an article cannot be sold.

return, *adj.* round-trip. One buys a single or a "return" ticket in Britain.

rhyming slang, *n.* a complex Cockney slang system, almost a tribal code, in which a phrase is used to stand for a word that rhymes with it, or, usually, the first part of a phrase. For instance, "head" becomes "loaf of bread" or, these days, "loaf."

ring up, *v.* telephone.

rise, *n.* a raise in salary.

rissole, *n.* a fried cake of minced food, usually leftover meat.

rock cake, *n.* a small cake with a rough surface containing currants.

rock salmon, *n.* dogfish.

roger, *v.* (colloq.) to screw, have sexual intercourse with.

roll neck, *adj.* turtleneck.

Rotten Row, *prop. n.* the track in London's Hyde Park set aside for horseback riding.

rotter, *n.* a term of abuse, strictly speaking a rotten person. An upper-class word, which is also public school (in the British sense) slang.

round, *n.* a delivery route, as in "milk round," "newspaper round," etc. Also, **roundsman,** *n.* any delivery man with a regular route.

roundabout, *n.* 1. traffic circle. 2. carousel.

rounders, *n.* a children's game similar to stickball, a version of baseball.

rowing boat, *n.* rowboat.

rozzer, *n.* (colloq.) policeman. Working-class.

rubber, *n.* eraser. The present deputy headmistress of a London school spent some time teaching in California, and once told a class going in for a geometry exam to be sure to have rubbers with them since anyone can make a mistake. She couldn't understand why this broke them up.

ruby, *n.* the 5½-point type known in America as agate.

ruddy, *adj.* (colloq.) an all-purpose adjective, synonymous with "bloody," but Prince Philip has

used it on television (on May 13, 1956), so it is widely acceptable.

rugby, *n.* a game superficially similar to American football in that it is played with the same shape ball and the object is to carry it to the end zone, but with many differences, including the size of the team, 15. Sometimes called **rugger.** It got its name because it originated at Rugby School.

rum, *adj.* odd, curious.

rumble, *v.* to find out about something, learn a secret.

runner bean, *n.* similar to a French bean, only coarser and thicker.

rural dean, *n.* a Church of England clergyman with authority over several parishes, ranking just below an archdeacon.

rusticate, *v.* to suspend a student from a college or university.

sailing boat, *n.* a sailboat.

saloon, *n.* a sedan car.

saloon bar, *n.* one of the two or more bars into which most pubs are divided, in class terms slightly superior to the public bar.

salt beef, *n.* corned beef.

Samuel Smiles, *prop. n.* the Victorian author of a book called *Self Help,* which preached the virtues of self-improvement, upright behavior, etc. He is often cited as the epitome of complacent Victorian attitudes.

Sandhurst, *prop. n.* the army academy, Britain's West Point.

sandpit, *n.* sandbox.

sanitary towel, *n.* sanitary napkin.

Sassenach, *n.* the Scottish term for an Englishman; originally the Gaelic word for "Saxon," it is now used facetiously more often than not.

saveloy, *n.* a highly-seasoned sausage.

Savile Row, *prop. n.* the street in London that contains most of the top tailors, hence the term for high-class, expensive tailoring.

savoury, *n.* a course in a meal, a light tasty dish usually offered in sophisticated English restaurants instead of a dessert or, occasionally, after the dessert.

savoy, *n.* a cabbage with a large close head and wrinkled leaves.

scale, *n.* a schedule of professional fees laid down by statute or by a professional body, e.g., certain lawyers' and architects' fees.

scarper, *v.* (colloq.) run away.

scent, *n.* perfume. Both words are used.

schooner, *n.* a large sherry or port glass, hence much smaller than an American schooner.

scoff, *v.* (colloq.) to gobble down, eat.

Scot, *prop. n.* the correct name for a native of Scotland. **Scottish** is the adjective to describe things

that come from there. **Scotch** should be used only about the whisky, strictly speaking, though this is not always adhered to, as the term that follows will show.

Scotch egg, *n.* a hard-boiled egg encased in fried sausage meat. A favorite cold snack in pubs.

Scotland Yard, *prop. n.* the headquarters of the Metropolitan (i.e., London) police. It used to be located on a tiny street off Whitehall called New Scotland Yard. Now it is in a modern building about half a mile away, but has still kept the same name.

scouse, *n.* and *adj.* (colloq.) referring to Liverpool or someone who comes from there. It also means a stew eaten locally and it derives from this.

scrag end, *n.* the cheap end of a piece of meat. **scraggy,** *adj.* meager, scrawny.

screw, *n.* a salary. An Englishman who says he is getting a good screw is talking only about money.

scrounge, *v.* (colloq.) to beg or borrow something. Used mostly in a lightweight sense, e.g., "Can I scrounge a cigarette from you?"

scrubber, *n.* a scruffy girl who sleeps around. A term of contempt.

scrum, *n.* the moment in **rugby** (see) when the forwards of the two teams, heads down, all push against one another. Occasionally used of social situations resembling this.

scrump, *n.* to pilfer fruit from fruit trees.

scrumpy, *n.* rough country cider.

scrutineer, *n.* canvasser of votes.

scullery, *n.* a room off the kitchen in large old-fashioned houses for rough cleaning work, like scrubbing pots and pans.

scupper, *v.* (colloq.) to ditch, sink, or cause to fail, e.g., "That's scuppered our plans."

season ticket, *n.* commuter ticket.

secondary modern school, *n.* the less academic of the two kinds of schools into which most of British secondary education is divided from the age of 11 onward. See also **grammar school.**

semi-breve, *n.* whole note. Musical.

semi-detached, see **detached.**

seminary, *n.* in Britain, a college for training Roman Catholic priests. It is not used about any other denomination.

semi-quaver, *n.* sixteenth note. Musical.

semolina, *n.* the large, hard part of wheat grains, used for making puddings.

send down, *v.* to expel or suspend from university.

send up, *v.* to mock or parody. Sophisticated slang, theatrical, etc.

senior service, *n.* the Royal Navy.

Also sometimes the **silent service.**

sergeant major, *n.* the highest rank of n.c.o. in the British Army.

service flat, *n.* a rented apartment which is cleaned and serviced.

serviette, *n.* table napkin. Alan Ross (see Introduction) says it is non-U.

shadow cabinet, *n.* the leaders of the opposition party in Parliament, who would form the cabinet if the opposition gained power. Each member has an area of responsibility, so that there is a shadow foreign secretary, a shadow defense minister, and so on.

shakedown, *n.* a makeshift bed for the night.

shandy, *n.* a thirst-quenching drink consisting of beer mixed with either lemonade or ginger beer.

shares, *n.* stocks. Though Britons speak of the stock exchange and a stockbroker, it's shares, shareholder, and the shares market.

shemozzle, *n.* (colloq.) fight, row.

shepherds pie, *n.* a pie of ground meat covered with mashed potato.

shilling, *n.* obsolete, strictly speaking, since decimal coinage was introduced in 1971, this refers to the coin that is now fivepence (it was 12 pennies under the old system); the word is still widely used.

shire, *n.* a county, usually applied to the rural aspects.

shoot, *v.* to hunt with a gun. An Englishman will say "I went shooting yesterday."

shooting brake, *n.* a station wagon with a large space at the back for luggage.

shop, *n.* store. "Store" is used only for a department or general store.

shop, *v.* (colloq.) to turn over someone to the police. Mostly an underworld term.

shop assistant, *n.* sales clerk.

shop fitter, *n,* a person who installs furnishings and display equipment in a store.

shop steward, *n.* the n.c.o. of the labor unions, elected by the men on the factory floor to look after their interests.

short, *n.* in a pub, this means a drink of spirits as opposed to beer.

shorthand-typist, *n.* stenographer.

shower, *n.* (colloq.) a stupid, disagreeable, or otherwise inferior individual or collection of people. Officers' mess slang, usually said in traditional officers' mess accents.

shufti, *n.* (colloq.) a look at something. An Arabic word brought back by the army. Heedless of the tautology, the services call some complex optical devices "the shuftiscope."

shy, *v.* to throw at something. A **coconut shy** is a traditional fair game in which you shy wooden balls at coconuts.

sick, *adj.* nauseous. To "be sick" means to throw up. It never means to be ill in any other way, though, illogically, Britons speak of "sick leave" and a "sick bed."

side, *n.* (colloq.) airs, a high-hat manner based on rank or position.

sideboards, *n.* sideburns.

silencer, *n.* muffler on a car.

silk, *n.* a lawyer who "takes silk" becomes a **Queen's Counsel** (see).

silver plate, *n.* as well as electroplate, this also means solid silver eating utensils.

silverside, *n.* the top of a round of beef, usually salted.

single, *n.* one-way. Ask for a railroad ticket and you will probably be asked "single or return?"

single cream, *n.* table cream, as opposed to double cream, or whipping cream.

sink, *n.* kitchen sink. The one in the bathroom is a basin.

six, *n.* in cricket, when the ball is hit out of the field so that it would be a homer in baseball; it counts for six runs. Hence, to hit someone or something for six is to score a resounding success. **Six of the best,** *n.* a spanking. A public school term.

skate, *n.* ray. This is eaten in Britain, and is often the fish in fish and chips.

skedaddle, *v.* (colloq.) scram, beat it. A schoolboy word.

skinhead, *n.* a young man with close-cropped hair, suspenders, and boots, which supposedly advertise a liking for thuggery.

skint, *adj.* (colloq.) flat broke.

skivvy, *n.* a maid, particularly one who does rough work.

skyve or **skive,** *v.* (colloq.) shirk, loaf on the job.

slash, *n.* (colloq.) the act of urinating, e.g., "I'm going for a slash."

slate, *n.* (colloq.) credit, e.g. "Put it on the slate."

slate, *v.* to criticize severely.

sleeping partner, *n.* silent partner in a business. Because of its obvious ambiguities, the term is being replaced by the American one more and more.

slog, *n.* and *v.* hard, plodding work; to persevere at this.

slow coach, *n.* slowpoke.

smackers, *n.* (colloq.) pounds sterling.

small beer, *n.* 1. one of several beers that come in a bottle smaller than the normal one and have a much higher alcoholic content. If you ask for a small beer in a pub, this is what you will get. 2. something of little account or weight. The term is used fairly widely today, but also has a long past, viz. Shakespeare, "She was a wight . . . to suckle fools and chronicle small beer."—*Othello.*

smalls, *n.* women's underwear, usually in connection with laundry.

smashing, *adj.* (colloq.) great, excellent.

the smoke, *n.* (colloq.) London, to people in central and northern England.

snakes and ladders, *n.* the commonest children's dice and board game. Because the counters, on their way to the goal, zip up ladders with good luck or down snakes with bad luck, it is often used in the construction of metaphors.

snap, *n.* a children's card game played with picture cards in which a player calls out "Snap!" when two of the same kind appear. Hence, in British speech, a cry of "snap" means that something has been discovered identical with something else, e.g., in the British movie *Live Now, Pay Later,* two girls talking about a local Lothario:

> "What happened when you went out with him?"
> "What do you think?"
> "Snap."

snifter, *n.* a small drink.

snip, *n.* bargain.

snog, *v.* (colloq.) to neck.

snooker, *n.* a kind of pool, the only kind played in Britain. The game of pool as such is unknown in Britain.

sod, *n.* and *v.* (colloq.) a term of abuse: "You sod!" is roughly equivalent to "You bastard!" As a verb, it is dismissive: "Sod it!"

means "Screw it!" It is also used occasionally as an adjective, e.g., "This sodding job."

Soho, *prop. n.* a small area of central London devoted mostly to strip clubs, restaurants, and other forms of nightlife.

solicitor, *n.* a lawyer who usually handles the out-of-court work. A lawyer who regularly appears in court is a barrister.

Solicitor General, *prop. n.* the Government's law officer, who can prosecute on behalf of the Government. Next in rank to the Attorney General.

solo, *n.* two-handed whist.

soppy, *adj.* (colloq.) silly. A childish word.

spanner, *n.* monkey wrench.

spare, *adj.* (colloq.) distraught, or hopping mad.

spatula, *n.* doctor's tongue depressor; it means the kitchen utensil also.

speciality, *n.* and *adj.* specialty.

spigot, *n.* the winding part of a faucet, never the whole faucet, as in America.

spinster, *n.* in officialese, any unmarried woman. Some fresh-faced American girls in Britain are surprised to see themselves described on official forms as spinsters.

spit and polish, *n.* (colloq.) smartness on parade.

spiv, *n.* (colloq.) originally a wartime term meaning a small-time black marketeer, it means now a sharp, flashy person who lives by petty dishonest dealings. The adjective **spivvy** means a sharp, flashy way of dressing that implies this character.

spot-on, *adj.* (colloq.) on the button, just what's needed.

sprat, *n.* a very small fish like a miniature herring. "Use a sprat to catch a mackerel" is a common folk saying, meaning to give something in the expectation of getting something more in return.

squadron leader, *n.* a rank in the R.A.F. equivalent to major.

square-bashing, *v.* (colloq.) military drill.

square dress hook, *n.* L hook.

squash, *n.* a soft fruit drink, not carbonated, e.g., lemon squash, barley squash.

squiffy, *adj.* (colloq.) a little drunk; a genteel term. During the World War I political crisis in Britain, the coterie of Liberal Party politicians who supported Prime Minister Asquith were known as the "squiffites"; there is disagreement about whether this was a corruption of Asquith's name or a reference to his fondness for liquor.

squire, *n.* 1. the principal landowner in a village or district. In its strict sense, the term is now almost archaic, and is used often for humorous or sardonic effect, as in the term "squirearchy." 2. a genial term of address in some circles, like "Mac."

S.R.N., *n.* state registered nurse.

stag, *n.* and *v.* in the financial world, someone who buys new stocks and sells them again for a quick profit. Also, "to stag."

stalls, *n.* the ground floor in a theater.

stand, *v.* a politician stands for office in Britain, instead of running for office.

starkers, *adj.* (colloq.) stark naked.

starters, *n.* the first course of a meal. An informal word.

state, *n.* and *adj.* pertaining to the national government. In political discussion, it often means the opposite of what it would in America. For instance, a demand for more state control in a certain area is a demand for *more* power for the central authority.

Statute of Westminster, *prop. n.* the statute passed in 1931 which ratified the independent status of the dominions, and is a sort of constitution of the British Commonwealth.

S.T.D., *n.* subscriber trunk dialing (see **trunk call**), the system by which a telephone subscriber makes a long-distance call by dialing it rather than going through the operator.

sticky, *adj.* (colloq.) difficult or dangerous. A **sticky wicket** (see **wicket**) is a difficult situation.

stiletto heels, *n.* spike heels.

Stilton, *n.* a rich, blue-veined English cheese, more expensive than most.

stingo, *n.* an extra-potent beer.

stocks, *n.* bonds. This, at any rate, is the correct use of the word in Britain, but it is occasionally used more loosely to refer to equity shares, as it would be in America.

stone, *n.* 14 pounds, a measure of a person's weight.

stony or **stony broke,** *adj.* (colloq.) flat broke. A 1930s upper-class term that lingers on here and there.

store, *n.* department store.

stout, *n.* a dark, sweetish beer.

stroppy, *adj.* (colloq.) belligerent, spoiling for trouble.

subaltern, *n.* a second lieutenant.

sub-editor, *n.* a person on a newspaper who combines the functions of copy reader and rewrite man (neither of these terms is used in Britain).

subject, *n.* citizen of Britain. Britons speak of a "British subject," though an "American citizen."

subway, *n.* an underground passage across a busy road. It does *not* mean an underground train system. That's the "underground" or "tube."

sunblind, *n.* a sunshade over a window.

sundowner, *n.* an evening drink. A word brought back from the tropical colonies.

superannuated, *adj.* old-fashioned; or unfitted to hold a job because of old age.

supertax, *n.* surtax on high incomes.

supplementary benefits, *n.* welfare payments, usually in addition to pension or other benefits, where these do not provide enough money to live on.

supremo, *n.* a supreme commander, usually military or in administration.

surgery, *n.* a doctor's office. It also means the period during which a doctor sees patients, e.g., "He has a surgery in the mornings and most afternoons."

surrounds, *n.* the skirting in a house plus the edges of doorways and windows.

suspenders, *n.* sock or stocking suspenders only. The other kind are braces.

swan, *v.* (colloq.) to live it up at someone else's expense, to go junketing.

swan upping, *n.* an expedition to seize young swans and mark their beaks with a sign of ownership.

swede, *n.* yellow turnip; the word actually stands for Swedish turnip.

sweet, *n.* 1. dessert. 2. a piece of candy. **Sweets** means candy.

sweetshop, *n.* candy store.

swiss roll, *n.* jelly roll.

switch, *n.* 1. a piece of false hair that is attached to a woman's hair to make it longer. 2. a point or switch on a railroad.

switchback, *n.* a fairground ride on an undulating track.

swot, *v.* and *n.* (colloq.) to work hard at studies. Used as a noun, it means a grind.

ta, *interj.* (colloq.) thank you. Cockney.

table, *v.* in parliamentary language, this means to put down for discussion, the exact opposite of the American meaning, to set aside. At the 1962 Geneva Disarmament Conference, the American and British delegations spent a large part of an afternoon locked in argument about whether to table a certain British motion before they found out they were on the same side. The Americans kept saying, to the Britons' confusion, "But it's a very *good* motion. Why do you want to table it?"

Taffy, *n.* (colloq.) a Welshman.

tailboard, *n.* tailgate. Not used as a verb.

take on, *v.* (colloq.) to display great excitement or emotion, e.g., "Oh, don't take on so over such a small thing."

tallboy, *n.* highboy, the piece of furniture.

tally clerk, *n.* a clerk who checks a ship's cargo against a list.

tallyman, *n.* a man who sells things from door to door, and collects payment by installments.

tanked up, *adj.* drunk.

taproom, *n.* a bar in a hotel.

tart, *n.* 1. an open pie. 2. prostitute, full-time or part-time. An old English barroom verse goes:

It nearly broke the family's heart
When Lady Jane became a tart.
But they clubbed together and bought her a beat
On the sunny side of Jermyn Street.

tart up, *v.* (colloq.) to prettify.

tat, *n.* a small object that is shabby, tawdry, or worn. In the theater it means an actor's accessories. **tatty,** *adj.* means shabby, tawdry.

ta-ta, *interj.* (colloq.) goodbye. Working-class.

tea, *n.* as well as a beverage, a meal. Among the middle and upper classes, a midafternoon snack accompanied by tea; among the working classes, the meal the man has when he comes home from work, his supper (see **high tea**).

tea leaf, *n.* (colloq.) thief. Rhyming slang.

tearaway, *n.* (colloq.) a young tough.

teat, *n.* the nipple on a baby's bottle. A nipple in Britain always refers to a woman's breast. Dr. Benjamin Spock's advice in *Baby and Child Care,* which is read almost as widely in Britain as in America, about widening the hole in the nipple by inserting a sharp needle caused some confusion and some mental anguish among British mothers, but, so far as is known, no physical injury.

Tele-cine, *n.* a film chain, the device which both projects and transmits TV film.

teleprinter, *n.* teletypewriter.

telly, *n.* (colloq.) television. Working-class.

ten-pin bowling, *n.* bowling.

terrace, *n.* a row of houses joined together. **terraced house,** *n.* one of such a row of houses, a term often used in real estate talk.

Territorials, *n.* the Territorial Army (or T.A.), part-time reserve soldiers.

test or **test match,** *n.* an international cricket event.

thick, *adj.* stupid, thick-headed, Also "A bit thick" is "a little too much to take."

thread, *n.* the thicker kind of cotton used for heavier sewing such as buttons.

through, *adv.* connected on the telephone. If a British telephone operator asks, "Are you through?" she means "Are you connected to your party?" not "Are you finished?"

thump, *v.* hit. Overheard in an East End pub:
"Wotcher, mate. Wot you been doing lately?"
"Three months for thumping a copper."

tick, *n.* (colloq.) credit, as in the phrase "The shop gave it to me on tick."

tick over, *v.* of a car's engine, it means to run with the gears disengaged; hence, in any activity, to go on operating but without making any progress. "The business is ticking over at the moment" means it's paying its cost but not making a profit.

ticket barrier, *n.* the entrance to a railroad platform or similar place beyond which you cannot go without a ticket.

tick off, *v.* (colloq.) to tell off.

tic tac man, *n.* a man at a racetrack who (quite legitimately) keeps the on-track bookmakers informed of the changing odds by hand signals.

tiddler, *n.* a very small minnow or stickleback; colloquially, a very small child, particularly one who is undersized.

tiddly, *adj.* (colloq.) a little drunk. A genteel, feminine term.

tied cottage, *n.* a cottage owned by a farmer and let to one of his farm workers for as long as he works for him.

tights, *n.* hose or pantyhose.

tin, *n.* can, e.g., Britons talk of a tin of peaches and a tin-opener. Also **tinned,** canned. But Britons speak of "canned music," not "tinned music," as Brian Foster points out in *The Changing English Language.*

tinker, *n.* 1. a gypsylike vagrant in Scotland and Ireland. 2. a mender of pots and pans; almost archaic.

tinkle, *n.* (colloq.) telephone call.

tip, *n.* a garbage dump.

tipstaff, *n.* an official in a law court who carries out certain court functions.

tipsy, *adj.* (colloq.) slightly drunk. A feminine word.

toad-in-the-hole, *n.* sausage meat baked in a batter.

tod, *n.* (colloq.) own, as in "I was on my tod." It derives from nineteenth-century rhyming slang, Tod Sloan (a famous jockey of the period) —own.

toff, *n.* (colloq.) a swell, big shot.

toffee, *n.* taffy.

toffee-nosed, *adj.* (colloq.) stuck-up, effete. Northerners often use the term about Londoners, their pubs, food, and la-di-da accents.

togs, *n.* (colloq.) clothes. **togged-up,** *adj.* dressed for the occasion.

Tolpuddle Martyrs, *prop. n.* martyrs of the British labor movement honored today; six farm workers of the village of Tolpuddle who were sent to a penal colony in 1834 for trying to form a union.

tombola, *n.* a lottery at a social function in which people buy tickets to win a prize.

ton, *n.* 2,240 pounds in Britain. Sometimes a 2,000-pound weight is called a short ton.

ton-up or **ton,** *n.* a speed of 100 miles per hour, achieved by a motorcyclist. It is used by Hell's Angels types.

top-drawer, *adj.* socially upper-crust.

top up, *v.* to fill a vessel that is already half full. One may, for instance, "top up" a drink, or a car's gas tank.

torch, *n.* flashlight.

Tory, *prop. n.* a member of the Conservative Party.

toss off, *v.* (colloq.) masturbate (male) .

tot, *n.* a measure of spirits.

tote, *n.* the equivalent of pari-mutuel, the racetrack's own betting system.

tower block, *n.* a high-rise apartment building.

town hall, *n.* the local government building of a city or borough.

trade union, *n.* labor union. The difference in terminology reflects a difference in labor organization. In Britain, unions are organized along craft lines rather than by industry. An electrician, a mechanic, and a carpenter working alongside one another in a railroad repair depot will belong to different unions because they have different trades.

traffic warden, *n.* a uniformed official who checks for parking offenses.

transport café, *n.* a cheap eating place on a highway used mostly by truck drivers.

transporter, *n.* a large truck that carries automobiles.

tram, *n.* streetcar.

treacle, *n.* like molasses only with a light flavor.

Treasury Bench, *prop. n.* the bench in the House of Commons occupied by members of the cabinet.

trendy, *adj.* voguish, ultra-fashionable. It's a trendy word.

trick cyclist, *n.* (colloq.) psychiatrist. A service term.

trillion, *n.* 1,000,000 billion, a million cubed. (See **billion.**)

trolley, *n.* tea cart.

trousers, *n.* pants. "Pants" in Britain means underpants. See Introduction.

trunk call, *n.* a long-distance telephone call.

tube, *n.* subway.

T.U.C., *prop. n.* Trades Union Congress, the national labor body.

tumble, *v.* to discover suddenly the truth of a situation. Unlike "rumble," this is usually used without an accusative object, e.g., "Then I tumbled."

turf accountant, *n.* bookmaker. A euphemism if ever there was one, this is the term they use to describe themselves.

turn it up, *v.* cut it out! stop it!

turn-ups, *n.* trouser cuffs.

twee, *adj.* icky, self-consciously cute.

twin set, *n.* a woman's sweater and cardigan to match.

twist, *n.* nervous flutter, as in the phrase "in a twist."

twister, *n.* a liar or otherwise dishonest person.

twit, *n.* a spectacular fool.

twit, *v.* to tease, josh.

U certificate, *n.* the equivalent of a G rating for a film in America, a license for the showing of a movie to anyone of any age.

U.D.I., *n.* unilateral declaration of independence. This term was first used when Ian Smith's Rhodesian Government declared U.D.I. in 1966, and soon became part of the political vocabulary.

uncle, *n.* (colloq.) a pawnbroker.

undercarriage, *n.* an airplane's landing gear.

underdone, *adj.* rare, about meat.

underground, *n.* subway.

Unionist, *prop. n.* the majority political party in Northern Ireland, which is committed to keeping the province a part of the United Kingdom (hence the name) and is affiliated to the British Conservative Party.

unit trust, *n.* almost the same as a mutual fund.

unofficial strike, *n.* wildcat strike.

urban district, *n.* a local government unit, governed by an urban district council. Not found in a metropolis.

u.s., *adj.* useless. The initials stand for unserviceable, and it was an army term originally.

utility, *adj.* this describes something that is simple and cheap while still performing its function; during World War II, the government, to save on materials, promoted "utility furniture" and "utility clothes."

V.A.T., *n.* value added tax, a complicated tax on products and services, which was first applied in the European Economic Community and introduced in Britain when Britain joined the Community.

V.C., *n.* Victoria Cross, the highest award for military bravery.

vest, *n.* undershirt. An American vest is a waistcoat.

verge, *n.* a grassy strip at the edge of a highway.

vet, *n.* veterinary surgeon. It never means a veteran.

vet, *v.* to check, to look over for soundness.

veteran, *n.* an old soldier or survivor of long service. It never describes a young ex-serviceman.

vicar, *n.* a Church of England parish clergyman.

villain, *n.* (colloq.) crook. Mostly an underworld and police term.

v-t, *n.* in television, videotape. In an American studio one would just say "tape."

waffle, *n.* and *v.* empty talk.

waistcoat, *n.* vest.

wallah, *n.* (colloq.) the person concerned with something, e.g., laundry wallah, accounts wallah. The word is Hindi and has a sound of the old empire about it, as do some of the ingenious applications, like "amen wallah" for clergyman, and "pop wallah" for teetotaler.

warden, *n.* the man in charge of

a residential institution, but not a prison. The head of a prison is a governor.

warder, *n.* a prison guard.

wash up, *v.* wash the dishes.

water ice, *n.* sherbet.

Webb lettuce, *n.* like an iceberg lettuce, only looser.

weir, *n.* a small dam across a river or stream; or else a fence for catching fish which strains the water rather than blocking it.

wellingtons, *n.* high, rainproof boots.

West End, *prop. n.* the center of London with most big stores and places of entertainment. Like most port cities, London spread out from the dock area in what is now East London, so that 150 years ago what is now the center of London was indeed its western end.

Westminster, *prop. n.* the part of central London in which Parliament and the principal organs of government are situated. The word is sometimes used to mean the center of government, or sometimes, the government itself.

wet, *adj.* (colloq.) used about a person, it means limp, silly, lacking in brains or substance—in a word, a drip.

whacking, *adj.* whopping.

whacko, *interj.* jolly good! splendid! Spoken in the accents of an (English) public school, and usually for comic effect.

whelk, a tiny shellfish sometimes eaten as a snack and sold on pushcarts at the seaside.

whip, *v.* (colloq.) steal.

whippet, *n.* a dog related to the greyhound. Whippet racing is a sport in some parts of England.

whip-round, *n.* (colloq.) a collection for a cause, worked up informally.

whisky, *n.* Scotch. This is what it is called. If any other kind of whisky is meant, it is specified.

whisky mac, *n.* a drink consisting of Scotch and ginger wine in equal proportions.

Whitehall, *prop. n.* the street in London leading from Trafalgar Square to the Houses of Parliament which contains most of the key ministries and the Prime Minister's official residence. The word is used often to mean the executive side of Government, including the bureaucracy, as distinct from the legislature.

white paper, *n.* a lengthy and detailed official account of government policy.

wholemeal, *n.* whole wheat.

wicket, *n.* in cricket, the three stumps behind the batsman which the bowler tries to hit with the ball. Also, the stretch of ground in front of it. A **sticky wicket** means, colloquially, any difficult situation.

wide boy, *n.* a professional cheat.

widgeon, *n.* a kind of duck.

wigging, *n.* a telling-off. Upperclass.

windcheater, *n.* windbreaker.

windscreen, *n.* windshield.

windy, *adj.* (colloq.) frightened. Someone who is windy has "got the wind up." Slightly dated schoolboy slang.

wines and spirits shop, *n.* liquor store.

wireless, *n.* radio. This word is a bit old-fashioned now, but it is still used. Some people objected to it when it was first introduced, like Lord Riddell, who said during a debate in Parliament on the first Wireless Telegraphy Act in 1923: "Why describe a thing as a negation?"

wizard, *adj.* (colloq.) excellent, very good. The term is dated, smacking of the 1930s.

wog, *n.* (colloq.) a nonwhite person, especially an Arab (pejorative). The word is said to be an acronym of "wily oriental gentleman." In some military circles in Britain in which global strategy is discussed, intervention in the Third World is known as "wog-bashing." British parochialism is often parodied with the phrase "Wogs begin at Calais."

Women's Institute, *n.* an association of women in many small towns and villages, genteel in style. Often shortened to W.I.

wonky, *adj.* (colloq.) broken, not in working order. Working-class.

woolsack, *n.* a cushion stuffed with wool on which, in accordance with tradition, the **Lord Chan-** cellor (see) sits in the House of Lords. The word is often used to mean the office of Lord Chancellor.

woolly, *n.* a sweater or cardigan. A homey, grandmotherly term.

works, *n.* factory or plant.

work-to-rule, *n.* go-slow; actually, a disruptive labor tactic that consists of working rigidly according to the regulations.

WRAC, *prop. n.* Women's Royal Army Corps, equivalent to the WAC.

WRAF, *prop. n.* Women's Royal Air Force.

wrap up, *v.* (colloq.) shut up.

WREN, *prop. n.* a woman in the Royal Navy. The word comes from the acronym of Women's Royal Navy.

W.V.S., *prop. n.* Women's Voluntary Service, an organization that does relief and welfare work.

Wykehamist, *prop. n.* an alumnus of Winchester, a leading public school (in the British sense).

Yankee, *n.* 1. (colloq.) Yank. Many a visitor from Tennessee or Georgia has been outraged to hear himself described in Britain as a Yankee. 2. at the racetrack, 11 bets in combination.

yard, *n.* a small area adjoining a house that is paved. If it has any grass at all, it is called a garden, however small.

yobbo, *n.* (colloq.) hooligan, thug.

Yorkshire pudding, *n.* a pudding made of unsweetened batter, to be eaten with roast beef.

zebra crossing, *n.* a road crossing marked in black and white stripes where a pedestrian has the right of way at any time.

zed, *n.* zee, the last letter of the alphabet.

zizz, *n.* (colloq.) snooze, nap.

American/British

abolitionist, *n.* an antislavery campaigner in pre–Civil War America; the antislavery movement.

adder, *n.* adding machine.

adjuster, *n.* (in insurance) an assessor.

administration, *n.* the cabinet and other officials appointed by a particular President. One speaks of "the Johnson administration" as one would "the Wilson government," though it includes more people. On the difference between British and American terminology, F. J. Goodnow, in his book *Politics and Administration,* offers this explanation: "The one, through its control of Parliament, makes as well as administers laws; the other merely administers laws made by Congress."

adobe, *n.* a sun-dried brick of earth or clay. Adobe houses are common in the Southwest. This is a Spanish word that has crossed the Rio Grande. Pronounced "a-doe-bee."

after, *conj.* past, as in "ten after two."

agate, *n.* the 5½-point type known in Britain as ruby.

aisle, *n.* a gangway in a store, church, or any other building: e.g., "The British fashion of having railway compartments instead of an undivided car with a nice long aisle."—from *Dodsworth* by Sinclair Lewis.

à la mode, *adj.* with ice cream.

alderman, *n.* a local official elected separately from councillors. In most localities in America, aldermen form a separate legislative body.

alfalfa, *n.* a leafy plant, related to the bean, grown widely in the United States and used as fodder. The approximate British equivalent is lucerne.

Alger, see **Horatio Alger.**

all-fired, *adv.* (colloq.) tremendously, extremely. An old-fashioned, rural-sounding term.

alma mater, *n.* one's old school or university.

alumnus, *n.* a graduate of a school or university. The Latin endings are preserved, so that the feminine is alumna, and the plural are alumni and alumnae.

ambrosia, *n.* a dessert of fresh oranges, bananas, coconut, and other fruits.

American Legion, *n.* the largest ex-servicemen's organization, nationalistic in its politics.

American plan, *n.* a hotel rate including meals.

angel food cake, *n.* a light, fluffy, plain cake.

Angelino, *prop. n.* a citizen of Los Angeles.

Annapolis, *prop. n.* the location of the U.S. Naval Academy, and in common speech the Academy itself; the equivalent of Dartmouth.

ante, *n.* the stake in a wager. The term comes from poker. **ante up,** *v.* means to put down one's stake. **penny ante,** *adj.* means cheap, small-time.

antebellum, *adj.* pre–American Civil War. One speaks of a southern antebellum mansion.

apartment, *n.* flat. **apartment house,** *n.* block of flats. **apartment hotel,** *n.* block of service flats.

Appaloosa, *n.* a hardy breed of horse developed in the American West, distinguished by its mottled colouring.

apple butter, *n.* a spiced applesauce served as a condiment.

applejack, *n.* a strong, home-brewed liquor distilled from fermented cider.

apple-pie order, *adj.* (colloq.) shipshape, in good order.

apple polisher, *n.* toady. The term comes from the custom in rural America of bringing teacher an apple as a present to win her favour.

applesauce, *n.* (colloq.) flattery, usually false.

area code, *n.* telephone dialing code.

armory, *n.* drill hall.

ascot, *n.* a broad scarf worn instead of a tie.

ashcan, *n.* dustbin.

ass, *n.* (colloq.) arse. A "piece of ass" is a common male phrase for a sexy or available girl.

assembly, *n.* in most states, the lower house of the state legislature.

assignment, *n.* homework. A teacher will say, "Have you done your assignment?"

attorney, *n.* lawyer. Both words are used equally.

audit, *v.* at university, to sit in on a course without the intention of taking the final exam or getting an academic credit for it.

auto or **automobile,** *n.* car.

automat, *n.* a restaurant where food and drink are obtained from coin-in-slot machines.

aviator, *n.* pilot. The most common term for an airman.

aviatrix, *n.* female of aviator.

Babbitt, *prop. n.* a smug, narrow-minded middle-class American. Also **Babbittry.** From the Sinclair Lewis novel of this name, which portrayed this kind of person.

backlog, *n.* this stands for the same thing in Britain and America but has a different meaning. In America, it means a comfortable reserve; an American businessman who says he has a backlog of orders is likely to say it in a tone of self-satisfaction. The word comes from the old log-fire days, and originally meant a log kept in the back of the fire as reserve fuel.

back-up lights, *n.* the reversing lights on a car.

bad-mouth, *v.* (colloq.) to disparage, speak badly of.

bagman, *n.* a collector for a crooked organization.

bags, *n.* suitcases.

ball, *n.* baseball. Also *ball park, ball player,* etc.

ball, *v.* (colloq.) to have sexual intercourse.

ballyhoo, *v.* to publicize with inflated praise.

baloney, *n.* a large, slightly seasoned Italian sausage, sold in delicatessens and popular as a sandwich filler. The word is an aberrant version of Bologna, for Bologna sausage. Used colloquially, it means nonsense, e.g., "That's a lot of baloney!" is a common dismissive phrase.

banana oil, *n.* soft soap, false flattery. Rare nowadays.

bang, *v.* (colloq.) to screw, fornicate with.

bangs, *n.* hair in a fringe.

bankroll, *n.* and *v.* a sum of money. As a verb, it means to put up money for some purpose; e.g., "Old debts were paid, dependents bankrolled, and h.q. funded." From *The Secret Army: A History of the I.R.A.* by Bowyer Bell.

barfly, *n.* someone who hangs around bars.

barkeep, *n.* a bartender.

barnstorm, *v.* to travel with a show or theatrical troupe. The term comes from the tradition of travelling players who used to perform in barns.

barrel, *v.* to travel very fast, e.g., "He was barreling along the freeway at a cool 90 an hour."

baseboard, *n.* skirting board.

bash, *n.* party.

bassinet, *n.* an infant's cot made of wickerwork or similar material with a hood at one end.

bat, *n.* a bender.

bathe, *v.* to bath. It doesn't mean to swim, though Americans speak of a bathing suit.

bathrobe, *n.* dressing gown.

bathroom, *n.* in America, this nearly always includes a toilet; hence the word is often a polite synonym for a toilet. If an American asks for the bathroom, he may want the toilet.

battenboard, *n.* perforated hardboard.

batter, *n.* the man wielding the bat in baseball.

bawl, *v.* (colloq.) cry, weep. **bawl out** (colloq.) to reprimand someone at length.

Bay area, *n.* the San Francisco Bay area.

bayou, *n.* a sluggish, marshy stretch of water, tributary to a river. Characteristic of Louisiana, where the word comes from, dating back to the time when the area was colonized by France.

bazooka, *n.* a crude, homemade musical instrument constructed out of a tube and tissue paper, invented and named by the 1930s comedian Bob Burns. The rocket launcher was so named because it looks like one.

BB gun, *n.* an airgun. **BB pellets** are the pellets fired by the gun.

beanie, *n.* a small, brimless cap, worn by youngsters.

beans, *n.* (colloq.) a small amount, as in "He doesn't know beans about it."

beast, *n.* (colloq.) an unattractive girl. An aggressive, insulting term.

bee, *n.* a gathering to perform some task, in cooperation or competition, e.g., sewing bee, spelling bee (at school). An old-fashioned word.

beet, *n.* beetroot.

bellboy, *n.* page boy. A colloquial version is **bellhop.**

belly-whop, *v.* (colloq.) to ride downhill on a sled on the stomach.

bench, *v.* to put someone out of action or out of the game. The term comes from football, where a player who is pulled off the field is sent to sit "on the bench," or is "benched."

Benedict Arnold, *n.* one of George Washington's lieutenants during the American War of Independence who went over to the British side; hence, another term for traitor.

berm, *n.* the strip of ground alongside a major road.

betty, *n.* a pudding open at the bottom, identified by its filler, e.g., apple betty, plum betty.

B-girl, *n.* a bar girl, equivalent to a nightclub hostess in Britain. She drinks with customers and is paid according to how many drinks they buy.

bill, *n.* a money note, as a dollar bill.

billboard, *n.* 1. hoarding. 2. in radio, an announcement of what is to come.

billfold, *n.* wallet.

billion, *n.* 1,000,000,000, or 1,000 million. A British billion is 1,000 times as much.

billy, *n.* truncheon.

bird dog, *n.* gun dog.

biscuit, *n.* similar to a scone.

bitch, *v.* (colloq.) to complain.

Though the word is used widely in its other, pejorative sense, both as a noun and adjectively ("bitchy"), this word in all its other uses is unisex. It carries no feminine connotation, and is used widely, for instance, in the services. **bitch up**, means to foul up or make a mess of a situation.

bitch, *n.* (colloq.) something disagreeable, e.g., "This job is a bitch."

black, *n.* and *adj.* Negro. "Black" is preferred among the modern-minded to "Negro" or "coloured" these days.

black-eyed Susan, *n.* a North American wildflower of genus *Rudbeckia* with dark brown centre and yellowish petals.

blackjack, *n.* (colloq.) a club or cosh.

blank, *n.* certain forms. Americans speak of a "telegraph blank."

bleachers, *n.* the cheap, uncovered stand at a sports stadium, so called because the occupants are "bleached" in the sun.

block, *n.* a city block bounded by streets on all four sides, or a stretch of street one block long. Distance in American cities is often measured in blocks.

block-busting, *v. part.* moving a lower-class family or several families into a block so that the other residents begin to move out, and the character and rental value change.

blooper, *n.* (colloq.) mistake, boob.

blotter, *n.* an official record of the events of the day, particularly at a police station.

blow, *v.* (colloq.) 1. get out, scram. 2. wreck, destroy, dissipate, usually in the abstract, as in "That blew all my plans," or "He blew his cool."

blowhard, *n.* (colloq.) a loudmouth, a person who talks big about himself.

blowout, *n.* puncture.

blueberry, *n.* an edible North American berry, resembling a bilberry, only blue in colour.

bluebook, *n.* a book listing the names of social prominent families.

blue-chip, *adj.* gilt-edged. The term comes from poker.

blue-collar, *adj.* pertaining to industrial workers, as distinct from white-collar.

Blue Cross, *n.* the largest private American health insurance organization.

Blue Grass State, *n.* Kentucky.

bluejacket, *n.* a sailor in the U.S. Navy.

bluepoint, *n.* the commonest kind of oyster served in the Northeast, much more common than oysters in Britain, caught around Blue Point, Long Island.

Board of Trade, *n.* a local businessmen's organization. It has no official standing.

boardwalk, *n.* a wooden promenade on the ground or sometimes above it, as along a seafront.

boat shoes, *n.* plimsolls with thick crepe soles.

bobbie pin, *n.* a hair grip.

bobby sox, *n.* brightly coloured, ankle-length socks. The term dates from the 1940s, when, for a while, a certain kind of teenage girl was called a bobbysoxer.

bobcat, *n.* an American lynx.

bock beer, *n.* a sweet, dark, German-style beer, lately become popular.

boffo or **boffola,** *adj.* smasheroo, a showbiz term indicating a resounding impact.

bohunk, *n.* an immigrant from Central or Eastern Europe, an unpleasant term. It is a combination of Bohemian and Hunky, or Hungarian.

boilerplate, *n.* material in a newspaper that is usable as spacefiller or dispensable.

boll weevil, *n.* a beetle of the American South that attacks the cotton plant.

bomb, *v.* (colloq.) to fail, to flop: used mostly in the theatre. The word has the opposite meaning to the same word used similarly in Britain. (See **bomb** in the British/American section.) Hence the double meaning in the title of Joseph Heller's play about a touring theatrical company with a play about a bomb-

ing mission which is and is not real, *We Bombed in New Haven.*

bonds, *n.* stocks.

bondsman, *n.* someone whose occupation is standing surety for people arrested and released on bail, at high interest rates.

boner, *n.* gaffe, resounding mistake.

boondocks, *n.* (colloq.) the backwoods, a remote rural area.

boondoggle, *n.* (colloq.) useless, time-wasting activity.

booster, *n.* a professional talker-up, singing the praises of something.

boot camp, *n.* U.S. Marine Corps training camp.

boozer, *n.* (colloq.) a drinker; never a bar.

Boston cream pie, *n.* a round cake with cream or custard filling.

bouncer, *n.* a chucker-out.

bourbon, *n.* whisky distilled from corn. Its original home was Bourbon County, Kentucky. Pronounced "burrbon."

Bowery, *prop. n.* a street in lower New York City, the centre of skid row.

boxcar, *n.* a goods waggon on a train.

box score, *n.* a detailed tabulation of results in a baseball game.

braids, *n.* plaits.

brakeman, *n.* a guard on a train.

branch water, *n.* water from a fast-flowing branch of a river or stream, which is therefore supposedly clearer and purer than tap water.

brickbat, *n.* a piece of a brick, particularly when used as a missile.

broad jump, *n.* long jump.

broiler, *n.* like a grill, only deeper.

Bronx cheer, *n.* a raspberry (the Bronx is a part of New York City).

Brooks Brothers, *prop. n.* in the style of this particular men's clothing shop in New York City, which provides smart but conservative tailoring, typically, for senior business executives.

brownie, *n.* a small, heavy, chocolate-flavoured biscuit, a children's favourite.

brown-nose, *n.* toady. A rather vulgar term, in its literal meaning scatological.

brownstone, *n.* a reddish-brown sandstone much used in urban building, particularly by prosperous people in the early days of this century; "brownstone house" is a common description for such a house, now often broken up into flats or furnished rooms.

brunch, *n.* a midmorning meal (the word is a combination of "breakfast" and "lunch") eaten usually on weekends, often as a social occasion.

buck, *n.* (colloq.) a dollar.

buck, *v.* (colloq.) to oppose a prevailing trend or force, as to "buck the system."

buckaroo, *n.* cowboy. A Western term. A corruption of the Spanish word *vaquero.*

buckboard, *n.* a horse-drawn cart with a raised seat for driver and passenger. Though it's seen more often in Western films, Steptoe drives what is very nearly a buckboard.

bucket shop, *n.* a crooked stocks-and-shares brokerage firm.

buckwheat, *n.* a grain used as fodder in Britain but for making various foods in America. **buckwheat cake,** *n.* a pancake made from this, a popular breakfast food.

buddy, *n.* (colloq.) a friend, a pal. It is a little small-townish, old-fashioned now. A favourite song of the Twenties went

> I don't want a girl, I want a buddy,
> 'Cos buddies never make you cry.

(In that innocent age, the sentiment was not thought of as perverted.) It is also used as a term of address, menacingly more often than affectionately, as in "Now look here, buddy . . ."

bug, *v.* annoy, irritate, as in "What bugs me is . . ."

bug, *n.* (colloq.) flaw, difficulty, usually used in the plural, and in a technological context, e.g., "It'll take a week to iron the bugs out of this project." This is one of several words that Dr. David Dalby, the London University philologist, has shown to have come into America from West African languages, having been brought over by slaves. (Others are *dig, jitters* and —this is more controversial, though Dr. Dalby argues the case persuasively—*Okay*.)

buggy, *n.* a small, four-wheeled horse-drawn carriage.

building and loan association, *n.* something like a building society.

bull, *n.* (colloq.) nonsense; an abbreviation of "bullshit."

bullhorn, *n.* megaphone.

bull session, *n.* a period of informal talk.

bum, *n.* 1. a tramp. This is one of those words from America that has now established more than a toehold in Britain and will probably be widely accepted soon with this meaning, rather than the anatomical one. 2. a general term of abuse, meaning just a no-good person.

bum, *adj.* bad, inferior.

bum, *v.* (colloq.) cadge, as in "Can I bum a cigarette off you?" To **bum around** is to knock about idly.

bumper car, *n.* dodgem car.

bumps and grinds, *n.* the gyrations of a striptease dancer.

bum's rush, *n.* the action of throwing someone out by the scruff of his neck and the seat of his trousers.

bunko game, *n.* a crooked card game.

bunt, *v.* and *n.* to tap a ball very lightly with a bat; a baseball term.

bureau, *n.* chest of drawers.

burlap, *n.* a coarse canvas, used for covering or sacks.

burro, *n.* donkey, a Mexican word.

bus, *v.* to take children by bus to a racially mixed school in another area, in order to achieve racially integrated schooling. The wisdom of busing is a major issue of contention in America.

busboy, *n.* commis waiter.

bushel, *n.* 2,150 cubic inches, instead of 2,219 cubic inches as in a British bushel.

bushwhack, *n.* 1. to travel through rough, bushy country. 2. to ambush in bushy countryside.

bushwhacker, *n.* during the Civil War, a Confederate guerrilla. Often used now for any guerrilla.

buss, *n.* and *v.* (colloq.) kiss. This is getting old-fashioned, and now sounds rather quaint.

bust, 1. *n.* and *v.* arrest. 2. a total failure, or to fail. 3. *n.* party.

butt, *n.* (colloq.) cigarette, also the end after it is smoked.

butter-and-egg man, *n.* a man out spending in a restaurant or nightclub. Also a well-known Louis Armstrong song.

B.V.D.s, *n.* a trade name for a kind of men's underwear, but once so popular in the western U.S. that for a while this word meant men's underwear.

caboose, *n.* the last waggon on a goods train.

cakewalk, *n.* a prancing walk that is part of a dance. Originally it was a feature of black dances, with a prize of a cake going traditionally to the best.

calaboose, *n.* a local jail. Mostly Western.

call, *n.* and *v.* telephone call. "I'll call you" from an American does not presage a personal visit.

can, *n.* a tin, as "a can of soup" or "canned fruit."

can, *n.* (colloq.) 1. toilet. 2. bottom, arse, e.g., "He fell on his can."

can, *v.* (colloq.) 1. to close off or shut off. "Can this talk" means "End this conversation." In the passive sense it can mean sacked, dismissed from employment. 2. to preserve food. A family "canning" peaches may be putting them into bottles.

candy, *n.* sweets.

Canuck, *prop. n.* (colloq.) Canadian, particularly French-Canadian.

canvasser, *n.* a scrutineer of votes. Quite different from the meaning in Britain.

Capitol Hill, *prop. n.* the hill in Washington, D.C., on which Congress meets in the Capitol. Used in political discussion, it is a synonym for Congress. Sometimes shortened to "the Hill."

car, *n.* carriage, as in railroad car and pullman car.

carousel, *n.* merry-go-round.

carpetbagger, *n.* a Northerner who went to the defeated South in the aftermath of the Civil War to exploit for profit, usually corruptly, the social and political disintegration. By extension, someone who sets out to exploit similarly such a situation.

carry-all, *n.* a car similar to an estate car, but higher, usually on a lorry chassis. *Webster's* says it comes from the French *carriole,* meaning a light carriage.

casket, *n.* in general use, a coffin. It means something else only if specified, e.g., jewel casket.

cater-corner, *adv.* or *adj.* in a diagonal or oblique position. Also catty-corner.

cathouse, *n.* (colloq.) brothel.

catsup, *n.* ketchup.

caucus, *n.* this has a more specific meaning than in Britain, meaning a small group of a political gathering that meets to take a decision. The word came to Britain from America, and is thought to stem from an Algonquin Indian word.

caucus, *v.* to go into caucus.

centennial, *n.* centenary.

Central Time, *n.* one of the four standard time zones in the United States, six hours behind G.M.T.

certified check, *n.* a check which contains a certification from the bank that the money is there and has been set aside for payment.

certified letter, *n.* a letter that is certified by a notary as proof of authorship. The certification does not relate to the contents.

chaparral, *n.* a thicket or clump of small trees, characteristically, in a Western desert landscape.

chaps, *n.* the leather leggings worn in the West for riding and ranch work.

Chap-stick, *n.* lip balm.

charlie horse, *n.* a stiffness in the leg, or sprain, or a blow that causes it.

charter member, *n.* founder member.

chaser, *n.* a long drink to soothe the throat after drinking spirits, e.g., "We were drinking rye with ginger ale chasers" or, from *archie and mehitabel* by Don Marquis: "If you will drink hair restorer, follow every dram with some good depilatory as a chaser."

chattel mortgage, *n.* a mortgage on movable goods.

check, *n.* a bill for food or drink. It also has the meaning of "cheque."

checkers, *n.* draughts.

check in, *v.* to register at a hotel.

checking account, *n.* current account at a bank.

check off, *v.* tick off.

check out, *v.* to leave a hotel, paying one's bill.

check-out counter, *n.* the cash desk at a supermarket.

checkroom, *n.* left luggage office.

cheesecloth, *n.* muslin.

cheezit, *v.* (colloq.) watch out! "Cheezit, the cops!" is a comic-book cliché.

cherry, *n.* (colloq.) hymen. The last cartoon in the American book *Fractured French* shows a bride leaving a church and waving over her shoulder with the caption "Adieu cherie."

cherrystone clam, *n.* a medium-sized clam.

chew out, *v.* to tell off, reprimand severely.

Chicano, *prop. n.* a Mexican-American.

chicken, *adj.* (colloq.) cowardly. **chicken out,** *v.* to back out through cowardice.

chicken à la king, *n.* chicken diced and creamed with pimento or green pepper.

chicory, *n.* the ground root of the plant, sometimes used to adulterate coffee. The vegetable itself is called endive.

Chief Executive, *prop. n.* the President of the United States.

chiffon, *n.* a dessert with a light, frothy texture, made with egg whites and flavouring.

Chinese checkers, *n.* a popular game played by moving marbles among holes on a board.

chips, *n.* potato crisps. British "chips" are French fried potatoes in America.

chisel, *v.* (colloq.) to cheat.

chocolate chips, *n.* specks of chocolate imbedded in a dessert, sometimes called polka dots in Britain.

chowder, *n.* a thick fish soup or stew, often with pork or bacon added.

chuck steak, *n.* slices of steak from the forequarters of the animal.

chuck wagon, *n.* in the West, a waggon carrying provisions for cowboys or farmhands.

chutzpah, *n.* (colloq.) colossal nerve. A Yiddish word. (See **stag.**) The "ch" is pronounced as a throaty "h."

cigar store, *n.* tobacconist's shop.

cinch, *n.* (colloq.) something easy to accomplish, a pushover.

city editor, *n.* a newspaper editor in charge of local news. It has nothing to do with finance.

cladding, *n.* much more limited than the term in Britain, this means only a metal covering on metal.

clapboard, *n.* overlapping planks.

clipping, *n.* a cutting from a newspaper or magazine, or, among gardeners, from a plant.

cloakroom, *n.* in Congress, a meeting place for gossip and informal exchanges. In a political context, "cloakroom talk" is the equivalent of "lobby talk."

closet, *n.* cupboard. Like a number of American words, this was current in Britain two centuries ago but is no longer used as a noun. A relic is w.c. for water closet.

cloture, *n.* a term used in political

assemblies for winding up a session or debate.

clout, *n.* influence, weight. Supreme Court Justice William O. Douglas referred in a historic opinion on the death sentence to the danger of "feeding prejudice against the accused if he is poor and lacking political clout."

club steak, *n.* a steak cut from the end of the sirloin; the wing rib to a butcher.

clunker, *n.* (colloq.) an old car; a banger, and an equally onomatopoeic word.

coaster, *n.* a small table mat put under a glass when serving drinks.

coat, *n.* it also means jacket.

co-ed, *n.* a girl undergraduate. It derives, obviously, from "co-educational."

coffee cake, *n.* not coffee-flavoured, but a fluffy, plainish cake sliced and eaten with morning coffee. Like a larger Danish pastry.

college, *n.* in common speech, synonymous with university. Strictly speaking, the word refers to an institute of higher education that does not have graduate schools. Thus Yale and Northwestern are universities while Swarthmore and Hamilton are colleges, though their bachelor's degrees have equivalent status. But someone who is studying at any of these will say he is at college.

Colonial, *adj.* pertaining to the first three-quarters of the eighteenth century in America, when Britain ruled the thirteen colonies, or the styles of that period, e.g., "Colonial-style furniture."

color wash, *n.* coloured distemper.

comforter, *n.* a quilt filled with down.

comfort station, *n.* a public convenience.

commencement, *n.* the ceremony of graduation from high school or university, so called because it marks the commencement of a new stage in one's life.

commercial paper, *n.* a promissory note that can be negotiated.

commissary, *n.* a store that supplies food and other goods in a mining camp or military establishment.

common stock, *n.* ordinary shares.

commuter ticket, *n.* season ticket.

Comstock League, *prop. n.* an organization famous in the last century for combating zealously sex or salacity in art and literature. Also **Comstockery,** a word introduced into the language by Bernard Shaw, after the society headed by Anthony Comstock had caused his play *Mrs. Warren's Profession* to be closed in New York. Shaw wrote: "Comstockery is the world's standing joke at the expense of the United States."

concert master, *n.* the leader of an orchestra, usually the first violinist.

concourse, *n.* an open space where people can walk and meet, often with shops, as at a railway station or on the ground floor of some of the large American office buildings.

condominium, *n.* an owner-occupied flat.

cone, *n.* a cornet, as in ice cream cone.

Confederacy, *n.* the union of Southern States in the American Civil War. **Confederate,** *adj.* applying to the Confederacy, e.g., Confederate troops.

congressman, *n.* though Congress has two houses, this always means a member of the lower house, the House of Representatives (as Member of Parliament always means a member of the lower house, the Commons).

Conservative Jew, *prop. n.* term roughly similar to Reform Jew in Britain in its limited deviation from orthodoxy.

cookbook, *n.* cookery book.

cookie, *n.* a sweet or semi-sweet biscuit.

cop-out, *n.* a get-out, an escape from some implied obligation.

copyreader, *n.* a sub-editor, one who edits copy on a newspaper and writes headlines.

cord, *n.* 1. string, wire, or flex. 2. a measure of timber, 128 cubic feet.

cordwood, *n.* wood cut into logs;

technically it means into a quantity totaling a cord.

corn, *n.* maize, or Indian corn.

corn bread, *n.* a bread made of cornmeal. Also, *corn cake, corn muffins.*

corn dodger, *n.* corn bread that is baked or fried hard.

corned beef, *n.* salt beef.

corn pone, *n.* a plain bread made of cornmeal, characteristically Southern.

cornstarch, *n.* corn flour.

corny, *adj.* (colloq.) stale, worn-out, applied to a joke, an entertainment, or an argument or attempt at persuasion. Also **corn,** *n.* corny material.

corporation, *n.* limited company.

cot, *n.* camp bed.

cotillion, *n.* a dance of the quadrille kind, or an elaborate ball.

cottager, *n.* someone owning or renting a holiday house at a resort. "It has ceased to be fashionable to bathe at Newport. Strangers and servants may do so, but the cottagers have withdrawn their support from the ocean." From *Their Pilgrimage* by David Warner, published in 1887, which shows also that weighty Victorian class distinctions were not confined to Britain.

cotton, *n.* 1. thread. 2. cotton wool.

cotton candy, *n.* candy floss.

cottonwood tree, *n.* a tree much like poplar with cottonlike hairs on the seed.

counselor, *n.* lawyer. This is a formal mode of address to a lawyer in some states. 2. someone who takes care of kids at a summer camp, an American urban middle-class institution.

counterman, *n.* a man who serves at a snack bar or lunch counter.

coupe, *n.* a saloon car.

coupon-clipper, *n.* (colloq.) someone who lives on an income from stocks and shares.

cowcatcher, *n.* a triangular frame on the front of an old locomotive, designed to sweep obstructions out of the way.

cowpea, *n.* a vegetable closer to a bean than a pea, grown mostly for forage.

coyote, *n.* a prairie wolf that inhabits the American West.

C.P.A., *n.* certified public accountant, the equivalent of a chartered accountant.

crab apple, *n.* a small, round, sour tree fruit, indigenous to North America, used in making desserts and jellies but not eaten on its own.

cracker, *n.* (colloq.) a poor white in the rural South.

cracker barrel, *n.* the barrel containing crackers that formed the central point of the general store in an old-fashioned small town, and in folklore, the centre of town conversation and gossip. It is used in expressions like "cracker-barrel philosopher," conjuring up a homey image.

crackerjack, *adj.* excellent, first-rate.

crack up, *v.* (colloq.) to fall about laughing. The verb can be either intransitive or transitive, e.g., "I just crack up" or "That cracks me up."

cranberry, *n.* a red berry used for making a jellylike sauce; cranberry sauce commonly accompanies turkey.

crankcase, *n.* in a car, the housing which encloses the crankshaft, connecting rods, and associated parts.

crap, *n.* (colloq.) excreta, but the word is not as nasty as it sounds. Like the French *merde,* it has left behind the scent of its true meaning. It means something with little value or else little truth. "The furniture is crap" means it is worthless. "That's a lot of crap!" means "I don't believe it."

craps, *n.* a popular American gambling game, played with dice. The spelling is changed when it is used in combination, so that one says **crap game** and **crap shooting** (playing craps).

crazy bone, *n.* funny bone. Both terms are used.

crib, *n.* a cot as well as a crib.

critter, *n.* (colloq.) animal. It is a corruption of "creature."

crosswalk, *n.* a pedestrian crossing.

crow, *n.* humble pie, in the expression to "eat crow."

crud, *n.* (colloq.) a term of abuse, mostly schoolboy.

cruet, *n.* not what it is in Britain, but a bottle for vinegar or sauce.

cube, *n.* a lump of sugar. Americans call lump sugar **cube sugar.**

cup, *n.* a unit of measure, 8 fluid ounces. Much used in cookery books.

cupboard, *n.* a kitchen cupboard, a place to store food.

cuspidor, *n.* spitoon.

cut, *n.* a block in printing.

cut-offs, *n.* jeans cut off above the knee with frayed edges.

dad-blamed, *n.* darned. Mostly rural.

dander, *n.* (colloq.) temper, as in "Don't get your dander up."

dandy, *adj.* fine, good.

D.A.R., *n.* Daughters of the American Revolution, a patriotic women's society, descendants of Americans of the War of Independence period.

date, *n.* an appointment of any kind; an evening out with one of the opposite sex, or a partner on a date; someone may introduce his or her companion as "my date for this evening."

date, *v.* to go out with someone on a date. **double-date,** *n.* go on a date with another couple, making a foursome. "I met Jack Kennedy in 1946. We were both war heroes and had been elected to Congress. We went on a double-date one night and it turned out to be a fair evening for me."—the opening lines of *An American Dream* by Norman Mailer.

datebook, *n.* pocket diary.

davenport, *n.* a large sofa. The word is Middle-American and slipping out of use.

daybed, *n.* studio couch.

Daylight Saving Time, *n.* summer time when the clocks are put forward an hour.

deacon's bench, *n.* a wooden seat for two, in Colonial style.

deadhead, *adj.* empty, used about a vehicle; e.g., "The truck carried four tons of concrete to Baltimore, and came back deadhead."

deadhead, *n.* (colloq.) one who attends a theatre, rides on transport, etc., without paying.

deck, *n.* 1. a pack of cards. 2. (colloq.) floor.

deck shoes, *n.* same as boat shoes, plimsolls with thick crepe soles.

deed, *v.* to transfer by title deed.

department store, *n.* a big store.

derby, *n.* a bowler hat. It also has the same sporting meaning as in Britain. It is pronounced differently, the first syllable rhyming with "curb."

devil's food cake, *n.* a dark, rich chocolate cake. It may sound like a Satanic concoction, but is harmless, and is served typically with coffee in the evening by homey old ladies.

diamond, *n.* the central, marked-out area in which baseball is played, actually a square consisting of a home plate and the three bases 90 feet apart.

diamondback, *n.* a domestic American rattlesnake.

diaper, *n.* nappy.

dick, *n.* (colloq.) detective. One of the most famous of W. C. Fields' films is called *The Bank Dick*.

dike or **dyke,** *n.* (colloq.) lesbian. A bull dike is an especially mannish one.

dill pickle, *n.* a cucumber pickled in dill water.

dime, *n.* a ten-cent piece. This is often taken in Britain to be a slang word, but in fact is the proper name for the coin and is written on its face.

diner, *n.* a cheap restaurant, usually with only a counter, often created in the body of an old railway carriage. Also, a restaurant car on a train.

ding-bat, *n.* (colloq.) stupid person. Mostly a youthful term.

diploma, *n.* usually a certificate of graduation from secondary school, called high school.

dirigible, *n.* zeppelin.

dirt, *n.* earth (it also means dirt). An American speaks of dirt-moving equipment, a dirt road, etc. **dirt farm,** *n.* a humble farm where the going is hard.

dirty pool, *n.* (colloq.) bending the rules, hitting below the belt. (See **pool.**)

dishpan, *n.* washing-up bowl. For

years, American soap manufacturers warned the country's womanhood of the miseries of "dishpan hands."

distaff, *adj.* female, in many combinations; e.g., "The distaff side of my family" means my wife and daughter.

district attorney, *n.* the public prosecutor for a district.

District of Columbia or **D.C.,** *prop. n.* the area in which Washington, the capital city, is situated, run by the Federal Government so that no state has sovereignty over it.

divided highway, *n.* dual carriageway.

Dixie, *prop. n.* the Southern states. Also, a song of that name.

dog, *n.* (colloq.) an insulting term for an unattractive girl, or any inferior thing or person.

doggie bag, *n.* a bag provided by a restaurant for carrying scraps of food home for a pet.

dogie, *n.* a motherless calf. First syllable pronounced to rhyme with "toe," second with a hard "g."

dog tag, *n.* a military identity disk worn around the neck.

donnybrook, *n.* (colloq.) row, quarrel.

doorman, *n.* the uniformed porter at the entrance of a building.

dormitory, *n.* a building that houses a number of students, a hall of residence. (See **dormi-**

tory in the British/American section.)

double-header, *n.* in baseball, two games played as a single event.

doughboy, *n.* (colloq.) an American infantry soldier; a World War I term.

doughnut, *n.* a ring-shaped pastry with a distinctive flavour. It is different entirely from a British doughnut, and not as sweet. It has no filling.

Dow Jones, *n.* the standard stock market report, issued in a teleprinter service by Dow Jones & Co., Inc.

downspout, *n.* drainpipe.

downtown, *n.* and *adj.* in the main part of town. But as well as being an area, it also means, in big cities where the streets are numbered, a direction. Thus a person in New York City at 181st Street might say, "I'm going downtown" if he is going to 42nd Street, or, to someone, "You walk three blocks downtown," directing him to a place on 178th Street.

draft, *n.* conscription.

drapes, *n.* (colloq.) opaque curtains. Net or lace curtains are always called curtains.

drawers, *n.* underpants.

drive-time, *n.* a term used in radio, meaning the morning or evening period when most potential listeners are driving to or from work.

dropout, *n.* someone who drops

out of school before finishing. Also, as in Britain, someone who drops out of society.

druggist, *n.* a man who dispenses or is entitled to dispense medicines at a drugstore; he is usually the owner or manager.

drugstore, *n.* a shop which dispenses medicines and generally fulfills the functions of a chemist, but sells also a wide variety of other goods, and normally has a counter at which snacks and sometimes meals are served.

drummer, *n.* (colloq.) a commercial traveler.

dry goods, *n.* textiles and fabrics.

dude, *n.* 1. a dandy, a man who lavishes great care on his appearance. 2. one unused to rough work.

dude ranch, *n.* a holiday place where beginners can ride horses and take part in other supposedly cowboy activities.

dukes, *n.* (colloq.) fists. "Put up your dukes" is a schoolboy challenge to fight.

dumb, *adj.* stupid. It rarely means "mute."

Dun & Bradstreet, *prop. n.* the common term for the financial reference book that gives the financial standing of all major companies.

duplex or **duplex apartment,** *n.* a flat on two floors, usually a luxurious dwelling.

dust bowl, *n,* an area subject to destructive dust storms.

Dutch, *adj.* (colloq.) in common speech, this often means German. (It is a corruption of *Deutsch.*) The Pennsylvania Dutch are descendants of German immigrants.

dutch oven, *n.* a flat iron saucepan with a cover used for baking.

Eastern Time or **Eastern Standard Time** or **E.S.T.,** *n.* one of the four standard time zones in the United States, covering the eastern part of the country. **E.D.T.,** *n.* Eastern Daylight Time.

eaves trough, *n.* another word for guttering.

editorial, *n.* leading article.

efficiency, *n.* one-room flat.

egghead, *n.* (colloq.) highbrow, an intellectual. The term was first used extensively during the 1952 presidential election, deprecatingly, about Adlai Stevenson. Stevenson issued the memorable clarion cry, "Eggheads of the world unite! You have nothing to lose but your yolks!"

eggnog, *n.* egg flip.

eggplant, *n.* aubergine.

eight ball, *n.* the black ball in pool, which should remain on the table until the last. Hence "behind the eight ball" means to be in a difficult situation.

electoral college, *n.* the body of electors who in theory elect the President, but in fact follow the dictates of the voting public.

elevated railroad or **elevated,** *n.*

sometimes shortened to **el**, a railway running above and along a city street.

elevator, *n.* a lift.

Elks, *prop. n.* a nationwide fraternal order. Mostly small-city middle-class.

Empire State, *prop. n.* New York State; the sobriquet was bestowed by George Washington and has been flaunted since then.

end, *n.* a position in American football, the last man on the line. An **end run** is an attempt to carry the ball around the end, and is often used as a metaphor for an outflanking manoevre of one kind or another.

endive, *n.* chicory.

english, *n.* a spin given to a ball when it is thrown or, in pool, hit with a cue.

English muffin, *n.* a flat roll for toasting, often eaten with butter and marmalade for breakfast. When my English wife visited an American drugstore for the first time with me, and I ordered breakfast, she was startled to hear the man behind the counter call out to the kitchen, "Let's have two toasted English."

enjoin, *v.* to forbid by law. The exact opposite of the meaning in Britain.

enlisted man, *n.* anyone in the service who is not an officer.

eraser, *n.* rubber. A "rubber" is a colloquial term for a male contraceptive.

Erector set, *n.* a popular children's toy, similar to Meccano.

ethnics, *n.* white Americans who identify with an ethnic subgroup, such as Polish-Americans or Italian-Americans.

European plan, *n.* a hotel rate for a room only, without food.

everglade, *n.* a tract of low, swampy land, characterized by clumps of tall grass and winding waterways, mostly in the South.

excise laws, *n.* the laws governing the sale of drink, tobacco, etc., when and how they may be sold as well as their manufacture, areas which in Britain are covered by the licensing laws.

explorer, *n.* a dental probe. The sharp instrument with which a dentist explores the teeth for cavities.

expressway, *n.* motorway.

fag or **faggot,** *n.* (colloq.) homosexual. Probably the most common term for this. Alistair Cooke, in one of his "Letter from America" broadcasts, recalled a conversation between an American and a British diplomat:

> AMERICAN: Do you know Lord —— by any chance?
> ENGLISHMAN: Yes, known him all my life. He was my fag at Eton.
> AMERICAN: Well! I'll say this for you British, you certainly are frank.

fair-haired boy, *n.* blue-eyed boy, favourite.

fair trade, *n.* subject to resale price maintenance rules.

fairy, *n.* homosexual.

fall, *n.* autumn. Both words are used.

fall guy, *n.* someone made to bear the consequences of something which was not his fault.

fanning mill, *n.* winnowing machine.

fanny, *n.* (colloq.) arse. The British film *Fanny by Gaslight* was called *Gaslight* when it was shown in America.

fatback, *n.* the fatty meat from the upper side of pork.

fat cat, *n.* (colloq.) a wealthy potential contributor to a cause.

faucet, *n.* tap.

favorite son, *n.* a candidate for national office proposed by a local delegation with local support.

fedora, *n.* a trilby hat. The name comes from the French play *Fédora* by Victorien Sardou. The famous actress Fanny Burney played the heroine in New York and wore a man's hat.

feisty, *adj.* (colloq.) peppery, temperamental.

Ferris wheel, *n.* the big wheel at a fairground.

field hockey, *n.* hockey. "Hockey" means ice hockey.

fifth, *n.* (colloq.) a bottle of spirits—it's a fifth of a gallon.

fig newton, *n.* a soft biscuit with a fig centre.

filling station, *n.* petrol station.

film chain, *n.* Tele-cine, a device which projects and transmits television film.

fin, *n.* (colloq.) a five-dollar bill.

finagel, *v.* (colloq.) to get something by devious means.

fink, *n.* originally it was a labour term for a blackleg or strike-breaker, now a general term of abuse.

finnan haddie, *n.* smoked haddock. Actually, this is the old Scottish term.

firecracker, *n.* firework. Both words are used.

fireplug, *n.* a fire hydrant. Both words are used.

first floor, *n.* ground floor. The second floor in America is the first floor in Britain, and so on.

First Lady, *n.* the wife of the President of the United States.

five and ten, *n.* the term for the big chain stores like Woolworth's, still used even though inflation over the past decades has made it an anachronism.

flack, *n.* (colloq.) public relations man.

flashlight, *n.* torch, To an American, a torch has flames.

flatfoot, *n.* (colloq.) a policeman. A genial word for him.

flier, *n.* a circular.

flip, *v.* (colloq.) to be carried away with excitement, in any direction, i.e., it might be rapture or anger.

float, *n.* an elaborate soft drink made with ice cream, similar to an ice cream soda.

flong, *n.* a papier-mâché mold used in printing.

floorwalker, *n.* shop walker.

flophouse, *n.* doss house.

flub, *v.* (colloq.) to botch up, make a mess of something.

flunk, *v.* (colloq.) to fail an exam or course.

flutist, *n.* flautist.

fly or **pop fly,** *n.* in baseball, a ball hit high into the air, easy to catch.

Foggy Bottom, *prop. n.* the area of Washington, D.C., in which the State Department is located, sometimes used as a synonym for the department.

folks, *n.* people or, more specifically, relations, e.g., "My wife's folks are coming over."

football, *n.* always American football, never soccer.

foreign service, *n.* the diplomatic service.

formula, *n.* a baby's liquid food.

forty-niner, *n.* a gold prospector who went to California in the great 1849 gold rush.

four-flusher, *n.* (colloq.) a faker, cheat.

Four Hundred, *n.* the social élite of a city. The term was coined in 1888 by one Ward McAllister, an arbiter of social distinctions who said there were only four hundred people in New York who really counted socially.

fox, *n.* (colloq.) an attractive girl. A newish, youthful term.

frag, *v.* (colloq.) to attack with murderous intent one's officer in the army. The term comes from the weapon most often used in such attempts in Vietnam, the fragmentation grenade.

frame house, *n.* a wooden house with a frame of weatherboard, more common in America than Britain.

frank, *n.* (colloq.) frankfurter, or hot dog.

fraternity, *n.* a club at American universities, the members ("brothers") of which are bound together by rituals and symbols. These are less significant than they were, and have vanished from some campuses.

freebee, *n.* something given away free.

freeload, *v.* (colloq.) eat and drink at someone else's expense. Also **freeloader,** *n.*

freeway, *n.* motorway.

freight car, *n.* goods waggon.

French fried, *n.* French fried potatoes, meaning chips.

French toast, *n.* bread dipped in egg and milk and sautéed.

fresh, *adj.* (colloq.) cheeky, impudent, as in "Don't you get fresh with me, young man," or, if the lady likes it, "Ooh, aren't you fresh!"

freshman, *n.* a first-year student. This is also applied to some other fields; one speaks, for instance, of a freshman senator, meaning one serving his first term.

fresh paint, *n.* wet paint.

funnies or **funny papers,** *n.* strip cartoons or comic books.

furlough, *n.* leave from the service.

G rating, *n.* a rating given to a film equivalent to a U in Britain, that is, anyone can see it. The G stands for general.

gabfest, *n.* (colloq.) a talking session. The phrase was first used in the early years of this century in an account of a long-winded session of Congress in the St. Louis *Globe-Democrat*. Since there are many German-Americans in the area, and the word is clearly coined from the German, it was taken up quickly.

gal, *n.* woman, particularly one working as a secretary or assistant in an office. If a professional man refers to "my gal," he means his assistant or his secretary. If he says "my girl," he means his girl friend or his daughter.

gallon, *n.* 231 cubic inches; a British gallon is 277 cubic inches. Pints and quarts have different liquid and dry measures in America, but a gallon is only a liquid measure.

galluses, *n.* wide, brightly coloured braces.

gam, *n.* (colloq.) leg. One of those words that are used more by film publicists than in conversation.

gander, *n.* a look at something.

gang bang, *n.* orgy.

gangway!, *interj.* called out as an order, this means "Clear a path, make way!" As in the line in Marc Connelly's play about a vision of heaven, *Green Pastures,* which Alexander Woolcott called the greatest entrance line in the American theatre, "Gangway, folks! Gangway for the Lawd God Jehovah!"

garage sale, *n.* jumble sale.

garbage, *n.* rubbish. **garbage pail,** *n.* dustbin.

garter snake, *n.* a common American snake, harmless, identifiable by three stripes along its body.

gas or **gasser,** *n.* (colloq.) something that produces happiness or merriment, like a party or a joke.

gas or **gasoline,** *n.* petrol.

gaslight, *v.* (colloq.) to drive someone crazy. From the play *Fanny by Gaslight.*

gassed, *adj.* (colloq.) drunk.

gat, *n.* (colloq.) gun. Mostly underworld slang.

gearshift, *n.* gear lever.

German shepherd, *n.* an Alsatian dog.

Gibson girl, *n.* the idealized American girl of the 1890s, as created by the illustrator Charles Dana Gibson.

Gideon Bible, *prop. n.* a Bible placed in hotel rooms in America by the Gideon Society, a society of Christian commercial travellers.

gimp, *n.* (colloq.) a cripple. **gimpy,** *adj.* lame.

gin, *n.* a machine for separating seed from cotton, the invention of which, in the early part of the nineteenth century, created the South's prosperous cotton-exporting economy. The word is probably a corruption of "engine."

Girl Scout, *n.* Girl Guide.

glad hand, *n.* a warm welcome.

glee club, *n.* a club for choral singing.

glory hole, *n.* a spare room where things are stored.

gob, *n.* (colloq.) a sailor in the U.S. Navy.

gobbledygook, *n.* (colloq.) jargon, difficult to understand.

goldbrick, *n.* (colloq.) a loafer, one who shirks work.

gold coast, *n.* a rich, residential part of town. More used in the 1920s than now.

gondola, *n.* a flat railway goods waggon with no sides or low sides.

Good Humor man, *prop. n.* the original ice cream seller who drove around, the company being the Good Humor Company. The term is now used often for any ice cream van salesman.

goof, *v.* (colloq.) to make a mistake.

goof off, *v.* (colloq.) avoid work, slack off.

goon, *n.* thug.

goose egg, *n.* 1. a zero. 2. a bump on the head; usually used about children.

G.O.P., *prop. n.* the Republican Party. The letters stand for Grand Old Party.

gopher, *n.* a rodent or ground squirrel found mostly on the prairie.

Gotham, *n.* New York City.

gotten, the alternative past participle of "to get," e.g., "I'd gotten a prize for English." It was British in Shakespeare's day.

grab bag, *n.* lucky dip.

grade, *n.* 1. a one-year stage in school. An American starts school at the age of 6 in the first grade, and leaves it 12 years later in the 12th grade. 2. a mark in school; a "good grade" in an exam means a high mark. 3. gradient. **at grade,** *adj.* at ground level. Used mostly in building.

grade crossing, *n.* level crossing.

grade school, *n.* primary school.

graft, *n.* corruption for gain in public office.

grand jury, *n.* a jury at a preliminary hearing.

grandstand play, *n.* something done to impress an audience.

greasewood, *n.* a low, stiff shrub found mostly in the West.

Green Mountain State, *prop. n.* Vermont.

green thumbs, *n.* green fingers.

gridiron, *n.* a football field, used often in sports reporting as a synonym for the game, e.g., "It was a weekend of gridiron thrills . . ."

grind, *n.* (colloq.) a hard worker. Mostly a college term.

grip, *n.* suitcase.

grippe, *n.* influenza.

grits, *n.* coarsely-ground grains of corn, wheat, or rice. A characteristically Southern food.

groundhog, *n.* a woodchuck, a species of marmot. **Groundhog Day,** *n.* February 2 or 14, depending on the part of the country. According to rural lore, this is the day that the groundhog ends its hibernation, and the day's weather is a sign of the season to come.

ground meat, *n.* minced meat.

ground round, *n.* best minced meat.

ground rules, *n.* the rules for a particular occasion. This is actually a baseball term, meaning the special rules for a particular stadium or field.

ground wire, *n.* earth wire.

G-string, *n.* a minute covering for the crotch, especially as part of an erotic dancer's costume. It did not always have this application, however. Mitford M. Mathews finds this in an account of Western travels in *Harper's* magazine in 1891: "Some of the boys wore only g-strings (as, for some reason, the breechclout is commonly called on the prairie) ."

guinea, *n.* an Italian or Italian-American. A racist term; street argot.

Gulla, *prop. n.* blacks living on a coastal strip in South Carolina and Georgia, and their dialect, which contains many West African words and hence is of interest to linguists. The word may be a corruption of Ngloa, the name of a tribe in what is now Angola.

gumbo, *n.* okra, a plant of West African origin, used as food. Also a kind of stew containing okra, identified by the principal other ingredients, e.g., chicken gumbo, shrimp gumbo. From Louisiana and thereabouts.

gumshoe, *n.* (colloq.) someone who moves about quietly and secretively, especially a detective.

gung ho, *adj.* (colloq.) aggressively energetic, very keen. It is a Chinese phrase that, during World War II, was the motto of an American Marine commando-style unit.

gut, *adj.* visceral, moved by primitive emotions, as in "gut reaction" and "gut fighter." **gut course,** *n.* an easy course at university.

gyp, *n.* and *v.* cheat, swindle. Used lightheartedly, or for small matters.

haberdasher, *n.* men's outfitter.

hack, *n.* 1. a horse-drawn vehicle, e.g.,

> Bring out your rubber-tyred hearses,
> Bring out your four-wheeled hacks.
> 'Cos I'm taking my man to the graveyard
> And I ain't gonna bring him back.
> —from the song "Frankie and Johnny."

2. (colloq.) taxi.

hairy, *adj.* (colloq.) dangerous, close to the edge.

half-and-half, *n.* 1. in a supermarket, a mixture of milk and cream, used in coffee. 2. in a brothel, an offering consisting of fellatio plus intercourse. The term puzzled many people in Britain when it was used by Jane Fonda playing a prostitute in the film *Klute*.

Halloween, *prop. n.* All Saints' Eve, October 31st, a festivity brought to America from Central Europe. It is associated with witches and hobgoblins, and children traditionally go around the neighbourhood creating mischief, or else threatening to unless they are given a present, with the demand to householders "Trick or treat!"

hamburger meat, *n.* minced meat.

handball, *n.* a game played by hitting a ball with the hand against a wall. An urban pastime.

happy hunting ground, *n.* heaven as envisaged by some Western Indian tribes. "He went to the happy hunting ground" is a cute way of saying he died.

hard-hat, *n.* construction worker, used as socio-political shorthand for manual workers with reactionary views.

hard-nosed, *adj.* (colloq.) tough-minded, hard-headed. There is no precise British synonym, but, oddly, an approximate antonym in "toffee-nosed."

hard-on, *n.* (colloq.) a male erection.

hard sauce, *n.* a sauce for desserts made with butter and sugar and, usually, cream and flavouring.

hard-shell Baptist, *n.* a fundamentalist Baptist, clinging dogmatically to traditional beliefs.

hash, *n.* 1. minced meat mixed with cooked potatoes and other vegetables, browned. 2. a mess.

hassle, *n.* quarrel, row.

haymaker, *n.* (colloq.) knockout punch.

hayride, *n.* a ride taken by a picnic party in a large waggon filled with hay. A common social event in rural America, and despite verbal associations, usually a decorous one.

hayseed, *n.* country bumpkin.

haze, *v.* to subject a newcomer to tricks or teasing.

heater, *n.* gas or electric fire. A fire in America has flames.

heavy, *adj.* (colloq.) serious, important.

heist, *v.* (colloq.) to steal.

Hell's Kitchen, *prop. n.* any district with a reputation for crime and violence.

help, *n.* servants, e.g., "The help will take care of it."

hemlock, *n.* a kind of fir or spruce tree, far from poisonous. American schoolchildren may not always know about the death of Socrates, but they all learn the opening words of Longfellow's "Evangeline":

> This is the forest primeval,
> The murmuring pines and the hemlock . . .

hero sandwich, *n.* a section of French loaf plus a lot of filling, making a huge sandwich.

hex, *n.* and *v.* malevolent magic spell; or to cast such a spell.

hick, *n.* and *adj.* rural or small-town, and unsophisticated, or such a person.

hickory, *n.* a native American tree of the walnut family, with strong wood. Andrew Jackson was known as "Old Hickory," because of his stubbornness and strength; traditionally, a schoolteacher's cane, when such

things were allowed, was a hickory stick.

high, *adj.* and *n.* a state of exhilaration, as, though not necessarily, caused by drink or drugs.

highball, *n.* any whisky and soda or ginger ale.

highboy, *n.* tallboy.

high-hat, *v.* (colloq.) to snub or treat condescendingly.

high-muck-a-muck, *n.* (colloq.) a person of assumed or real importance. The phrase takes him down a peg. It comes from the Chinook Indian.

high school, *n.* secondary school, covering roughly the ages 14 to 18.

high-toned, *adj.* socially refined, or perhaps snobbish.

hike, *n.* a boost, a rise; e.g., "Auto Workers Seek 9 p.c. Pay Hike." —New York *Times* headline.

hike, *v.* a motion in American football in which the centre flips the ball back between his legs to one of the backs, starting the play.

hipped, *past part.* fanatically keen, as in "He was hipped on astral consciousness."

hit, *v.* (colloq.) to turn to or take up; to "hit the road" means to go away or travel, to "hit the bottle" means to take to drink, to "hit the sack" means to go to bed. By itself, "hit it!" is an encouraging exhortation meaning something like "Go man go!"

hit, *n.* (colloq.) a murder; an underworld term.

hitch, *v.* (colloq.) marry. Used without an object, e.g., "We got hitched," never "He hitched her."

hockey, *n.* ice hockey, unless otherwise specified.

hogwash, *n.* (colloq.) nonsense.

home free, *adj.* home and dry.

home run, *n.* a hit in baseball that takes the batter right around the bases to score a run. Often reduced to **homer.**

homely, *adj.* plain featured, or downright ugly. This meaning has now overcome many others. More than one Englishman being entertained in an American home has startled fellow guests by describing his hostess as "a very homely lady."

homemaker, *n.* housewife. This word was introduced into the language by women's magazines over the past 25 years, in the belief that the word "housewife" implied a menial or subservient status. The change was not a precursor of women's lib, since it would change the status rather than the role.

homesteader, *n.* one of the settlers in the old West who took advantage of the Homestead Act, which gave away land in order to encourage settlement of the West.

hominy grits, *n.* boiled, coarsely-ground maize. A Southern and usually rural dish.

honky, *n.* (colloq.) a common black American term for a white man.

Honorable, *adj.* an honorific before the name of a senior office-holder, e.g., a congressman or state governor. It is never used for the President or a cabinet member.

honor system, *n.* the system at university by which students taking an exam are freed from any supervision and can come and go as they please, and sign a pledge that they have not cheated.

hooch, *n.* (colloq.) spirits.

hood, *n.* 1. a car's bonnet. 2. (colloq.) a gangster, abbreviation of "hoodlum."

hooker, *n.* prostitute.

hookey, *n.* (colloq.) truant. To go truant is to "play hookey."

hoosegow, *n.* jail. A Western word, from the Spanish *juzgado,* meaning "judged."

Hoosier, *n.* and *adj.* native to Indiana.

hootchy-kootchy, *n.* a strip-type dance, modest by today's standards but daring in earlier years. The term comes from the Orient.

hope chest, *n.* bottom drawer.

Horatio Alger, *prop. n.* the author of many boys' books around the turn of the century, in which the hero as a boy was honest, upright, and hard-working, and rose to wealth and success; hence the archetype of such a rags-to-riches story. "It had its Horatio Alger heroes and its robber barons, but no empire builders." From *Desert Challenge* by Robert Lilliard.

horn, *n.* 1. (colloq.) telephone. 2. the pommel of a saddle.

hornswoggle, *v.* to hoax, deceive, or bamboozle.

horny, *adj.* (colloq.) randy.

horseplay, *n.* friendly, male, rough-housing. **horse around,** *v.* indulge in horseplay.

hostler, *n.* ostler.

hotfoot, *n.* a savage practical joke which consists of attaching a match to a person's shoe when he is not looking and lighting it.

hot rod, *n.* an old car altered to give it much more power.

housing project, *n.* a housing development or estate.

Hoyle, *prop. n.* referring to Edmund Hoyle, an eighteenth-century Englishman more honoured abroad than at home, who compiled a book of standard rules for games; "according to Hoyle" means strictly according to the rule.

huckleberry, *n.* a North American fruit similar to a blackberry.

huckster, *n.* a hard-sell salesman. A fairground barker. Also used, ironically, for advertising executives.

huddle, *n.* in football, a brief conference of the team on the field to receive instructions on the next move. Hence, any secret planning conference.

humidor, *n.* cigar box.

hump, *v.* (colloq.) to fornicate. Fairly vulgar.

hundredweight, *n.* one hundred pounds, not 112.

hung jury, *n.* a jury that is divided and cannot reach a verdict.

hunk, *n.* (colloq.) a gorgeous, attractive man.

hunkered, *adj.* squatting on the haunches. Actually, an old Scottish word.

Hunky, *n.* (colloq.) an immigrant from Hungary.

hunky-dory, *adj.* (colloq.) fine, very satisfactory.

hunting, *n.* hunting with a gun.

hurdy-gurdy, *n.* barrel organ.

hush puppy, *n.* a small, deep-fried cornmeal cake. Southern.

hustler, *n.* someone who lives on his wits, a sharp operator who "hustles" for business.

iceberg lettuce, *n.* similar to a web lettuce.

icebox, *n.* still used for a refrigerator.

I.D. card, *n.* identity card.

incorporated, *adj.* limited, as in a limited company. "Inc." after a name is the equivalent of "Ltd."

Indian giver, *n.* (colloq.) someone who gives something and then asks for it back. A juvenile term.

information, *n.* directory inquiries, on the telephone.

installment plan, n. hire purchase.

instructor, n. a junior university teacher.

intern, n. houseman in a hospital.

Internal Revenue, n. Inland Revenue.

intramural, adj. within one school or university, as "intramural sports."

Ivy League, n. and adj. no actual organization, but the large, old-established universities in the Eastern states that are educationally and socially esteemed.

jack, n. (colloq.) money. "All work and no play makes jack." —from *Comfort Me with Apples* by Peter de Vries.

jackass, n. a male donkey. Colloquially, a stupid person.

jacklight, n. a portable lantern, such as is used in camping.

jacks, n. a game with a little ball and metal counters played by small children, often in the streets or playgrounds.

janitor, n. caretaker.

Jell-O, n. jelly. A brand name, but widely used.

jelly roll, n. Swiss roll. It is also, in Negro slang, a term for a fine detail of sexual activity, and it is from this rather than the bakery that the great jazz pianist Jelly Roll Morton drew his nickname.

jerk, n. (colloq.) a stupid person. A soda jerk, which has no pe-jorative connotation, is a man who serves behind the counter at a soda fountain. The phrase comes from the jerking motion with which he draws the drinks.

jerk off, v. (colloq.) masturbate.

jerkwater, adj. (colloq.) small and insignificant. Usually refers to a place.

jimmy, n. jemmy.

jitney, n. a local transport for short journeys.

jockstrap or jock, n. (colloq.) a keen athlete. Mostly a campus and service term.

john, n. (colloq.) toilet.

John Doe, prop. n. 1. an average American. 2. a person of unknown identity in legal proceedings. In this case, the unknown person is entered in court records as John Doe.

John Hancock, n. (colloq.) signature. Derives from the fact that John Hancock's is the first signature on the American Declaration of Independence.

joiner, n. someone with a propensity for joining clubs and other organizations.

josh, v. (colloq.) to tease, subject to light banter.

jug, n. and v. (colloq.) jail.

jumper, n. a loose outer jacket, usually worn over clothes to protect them.

jumping rope, n. skipping rope.

June bug, n. any of various large beetles of the genus *Phyllophaga*.

jungle bunny, *n.* (colloq.) Negro. An insult. The term has been given wide currency by Archie Bunker, the character in the TV comedy series "All in the Family" modeled on Britain's Alf Garnett.

junior, *n.* a student in the third year of his or her four-year course at secondary school or university.

junior college, *n.* an educational institution that offers studies equivalent to the first two years at university, and also, often, adult education.

justice of the peace, *n.* an official similar to a J.P. in Britain except that he can also perform marriages. Hence in romantic story and song, to go and look for a justice of the peace means to set out to get married.

kaffeeklatsch, *n.* a social gathering for coffee and chat.

kazoo, *n.* a crude, homemade musical instrument, consisting of a tube with a taut wire. A child's toy.

kerosene, *n.* paraffin.

kettle, *n.* a metal vessel for boiling liquid. The particular kind that is a kettle in Britain is called a **tea kettle.**

key punch, *n.* card punch.

kibbitz, *v.* (colloq.) to give advice, requested or not, as to a player in a card game. Like many American colloquialisms, this comes from Yiddish. It is not to be confused with a collective settlement in Israel.

kickback, *n.* (colloq.) money that is paid illicitly in a business deal. If a buyer for a firm places a large order with a company in return for a bribe of 2% of the price of the order, that 2% is the kickback.

kicks, *n.* shoes. Used mostly by young people.

kitchen cabinet, *n.* a close group of Presidential advisers chosen on a personal basis.

knickers, *n.* baggy trousers tucked in below the knee. They were standard boy's wear in America for many years and are still seen.

knock up, *v.* (colloq.) to get with child. A British girl visiting America told friends throughout one day that she was tired because the hotel porter had knocked her up early in the morning. The responses varied from "Gee, that's awful!" to "But how can you tell so *soon?*"

Know-Nothings, *n.* historically, the Native American Party in the mid-nineteenth century, dedicated to preserving American virtues against immigration and Roman Catholicism. It was conspiratorial in style, and takes its nickname from the insistence of officers when questioned that they knew nothing of its organization. The term is sometimes used in political abuse today.

kook, *n.* an eccentric person; not necessarily pejorative.

kooky, *adj.* eccentric, nutty.

k.p. *or* **kitchen police,** *n.* an assignment to clean in the kitchens. A service term.

Labor Day, *prop. n.* the first Monday in September, always a national holiday. For most Americans, the three-day Labor Day weekend marks the end of summer.

labor union, *n.* trade union (for a note on the significance of the difference in terminology, see **trade union** in the British/American section) .

ladybug, *n.* ladybird.

lame duck, *n.* and *adj.* in politics, a person whose term of office is due to end soon, and who has therefore lost some of his authority. A lame duck President is one whose successor has already been elected.

landing gear, *n.* an airplane's undercarriage.

land patent, *n.* title deed to a plot of land.

lay, *v.* to have sexual intercourse with. The verb can be used in either direction, i.e., "He lays her" or "She lays him." The classic double entendre employing this word is Dorothy Parker's "If all the girls who ever danced in the Ziegfeld Follies were laid end to end, I wouldn't be surprised."

leader, *n.* an article for sale in a shop or supermarket in order to tempt customers to buy other things. **loss leader,** *n.* an article that is sold below cost for this purpose.

leatherneck, *n.* a U.S. Marine. Seen mostly in newspapers.

letter, *n.* in campus terminology, the initial of the university on a sweater, denoting that the person is a member of a sports team. Getting it is an achievement.

levee, *n.* an embankment on a river built to prevent flooding. As the song goes: "Waitin' on the levee, waitin' for the *Robert E. Lee."*

leverage, *n.* gearing. The ratio between a company's capital and money borrowed. A financial term.

L hook, *n.* a square dress hook.

liberal, *adj.* politically, anyone on the reformist left wing, not so far left as a radical. There is no Liberal Party in national American politics.

license plate, *n.* a number plate on a car.

life preserver, *n.* life jacket or life belt.

lightning bug, *n.* glowworm.

lily, *n.* (colloq.) a sissy, a weak or effeminate man.

lima bean, *n.* a common vegetable, like a broad bean only more delicate.

limit line, *n.* the solid white line

on a road delineating a pedestrian crossing.

limp-wrist, *n.* and *adj.* (colloq.) homosexual.

liquor store, *n.* wines and spirits shop.

liverwurst, *n.* liver sausage.

loaded, *adj.* (colloq.) 1. rich. 2. drunk.

loafer, *n.* a loose shoe without laces, a casual.

local, *n.* trade union branch.

locate, *v.* to settle in a home or job. "Are you located yet?" to a new arrival means "Have you got a place to live?" or "Have you found a job?"

loco, *adj.* crazy. **locoweed,** *n.* a weed found in the Southwest which gives animals brain disease when they eat it.

loge, *n.* the front of the dress circle at the theatre.

log roll, *v.* to do a favour in return for a favour. Used often in politics. It comes from the pioneering days; a man could chop down trees and saw them up into logs to build his cabin, but could not roll them to the site himself. He would solicit his neighbour's help on the basis of "You help roll my logs and I'll help roll yours."

Lone Star State, *n.* Texas. The phrase comes from the state flag, and the single star marks the fact that Texas was an independent republic for ten years, from 1836.

long-distance call, *n.* a trunk telephone call.

longshoreman, *n.* a docker, who loads and unloads ships.

lot, *n.* a plot of land. Often used in combination, e.g., sandlot, parking lot.

lowboy, *n.* a low dressing table with drawers.

luau, *n.* a Hawaiian barbecue, a form of social entertaining.

lulu or **looloo,** *n.* (colloq.) something extraordinary in some way or another. "That's a lulu!" means the same as "That's really something!"

lumber, *n.* timber. **lumberjack,** *n.* a man who cuts down trees.

lumberjacket, *n.* a heavy woolen jacket.

lumps, *n.* (colloq.) metaphorically, bruises. If someone loses badly in a game or other situation, it may be said that he "got his lumps."

lunch pail, *n.* the container in which a workman takes his lunch to work.

lunkhead, *n.* (colloq.) a thick-headed person.

lush, *n.* (colloq.) a drunkard.

M rating, *n.* a rating given to a film equivalent to an A in Britain. It means that parents may find the film unsuitable for children. The M stands for "mature."

Mac, *n.* (colloq.) a common, informal form of address to someone who is not known by name, used similarly to "sport" or "squire" in Britain. An American I know once said to the bartender in a British pub, "Let me have a large whisky, Mac," and was given a whisky mac.

Mace, *n.* a riot gas used by many American police forces similar to C.S. gas.

mackinaw, *n.* a short woolen coat, as worn by hunters in the northern woods.

mad, *adj.* (colloq.) angry. It is usually used in a light vein rather than about very serious or weighty matters. Grammatically, it is used as an exact equivalent of "angry," e.g., "He'll get mad if he hears about it," never "He'll go mad."

Madison Avenue, *prop. n.* the advertising world. This is actually a New York City street that contains many advertising agencies.

mad money, *n.* money that a girl may keep in reserve when she goes out with a man in case she "gets mad" at him and has to make her own way home.

maid of honor or **matron of honor,** *n.* the bride's principal attendant at a wedding ceremony, customarily a sister or close friend.

mail, *n.* post, also **mailman, mailbox** (the latter has two meanings: the box where one posts letters, and the box outside a home where letters are delivered). But the service is the post office, and so is the place.

Main Street, *prop. n.* the high street; the term often stands for small-town America.

major, *n.* at university, one's subject of principal study; sometimes used about a student, e.g., "She was a crazy mathematics major from the Wharton School of Business who could not count to 28 each month without getting into trouble." From *Catch-22* by Joseph Heller.

make, *v.* 1. to get into, as "He made the football team" or "He made the *Daily News* sports page." 2. seduce.

makefast, *n.* any structure to which a ship or boat is tied up.

make out, *v.* (colloq.) to succeed sexually.

Malamute, *prop. n.* an Eskimo tribe. Also, a breed of dog from Alaska.

malted milk or **malted,** *n.* a sweet, rich drink made of milk, ice cream, flavouring, and malt powder.

Manhattan, *prop. n.* 1. the island that is the central part of New York City. 2. a popular American cocktail made of rye whisky, vermouth, and bitters, served with a cherry.

manifest destiny, *n.* the doctrine promulgated first in the 1840s that it was the "manifest destiny"—the phrase was first used by a statesman of the period, John O'Sullivan—of the American people to govern the American continent; it was later extended by some to cover the destiny of the Anglo-Saxons to dominate the world.

Mann Act, *prop. n.* an act of Congress that declares it a federal offense to take a woman across a state line for what in those days was termed "immoral purposes." It is still in effect.

maple sugar, maple syrup, *n.* sugar and syrup made in New England from the sap of maple trees, with a distinct and delicious flavour.

market, *v.* to shop. An American housewife will say, "I'm going to do some marketing."

martini, *n.* the most popular American cocktail, often called a "dry martini" made of three (or more) parts gin to one part dry vermouth, usually served with an olive. Among other fulsome tributes: "The proper union of gin and vermouth is a great and sudden glory; it is one of the happiest marriages on earth."—Bernard de Voto.

mason, *n.* anyone who works with stone or bricks.

Mason-Dixon line, *prop. n.* the traditional dividing line between the Northern and Southern states, actually the southern boundary of Pennsylvania. Used frequently in a geographical, political, or social context. It is named after two English surveyors who drew the line in the 1760s, Charles Mason and Jeremiah Dixon.

Masonite, *n.* fiberboard. This is a brand name that has become a part of the language.

match, *v.* to match coins or bills in a kind of heads-or-tails game.

maverick, *n.* a cow that does not have the brand of one herd. Hence, by extension, anyone who stands apart from a group, such as a political party, and takes a solitary stance.

mayor, *n.* a municipal official elected directly, and with far more powers than a mayor in Britain.

mazuma, *n.* (colloq.) money.

M.D. (*abbr.*) *n.* medical doctor, a common term for a qualified physician.

mean, *adj.* nasty. It does not mean specifically stingy.

measure, *n.* a bar in music.

meat-ax, *n.* any crude instrument wielded with a heavy hand, e.g., an American reporter complaining: "He edited my story with a meat-ax."

meat loaf, *n.* a large, baked piece of minced meat, served in slices.

Medal of Honor, *prop. n.* the military's highest award for bravery. Also called the **Congressional Medal of Honor.**

mesa, *n.* a high, narrow plateau with steep sides, a feature of the landscape in much of the South-west. It is a Spanish word mean-ing "table."

mess hall, *n.* dining hall.

mess kit, *n.* eating utensils, in-cluding plates.

metallic road, *n.* a paved road, as opposed to a gravel road.

mezzanine, *n.* dress circle in a theatre or cinema.

mickey finn, *n.* (colloq.) a drink to which knockout drops have been added.

milk run, *n.* in airmen's slang, a successful, uneventful flight.

Milquetoast, *prop.* *n.* Casper Milquetoast was a comic-strip character who was the epitome of the mild-mannered weakling.

mini-bike, *n.* moped.

minor, *n.* in university, one's sec-ondary subject, the opposite of major, e.g., "His major was English literature, his minor po-litical science."

mint julep, *n.* a long, cool drink made with bourbon and mint, traditionally the drink of South-ern planters.

Missouri, *prop. n.* (colloq. use) a man from Missouri is, accord-ing to tradition, a skeptic who has to be shown something be-fore he believes it. Hence, "I'm from Missouri" means "I'll be-lieve it when I see it."

Mister Charlie, *n.* (colloq.) a Ne-gro term for a white man.

mitt, *n.* 1. a baseball glove, a huge padded glove made for catching

rather than throwing. 2. (col-loq.) a hand.

mixer, *n.* 1. a sociable, gregarious person. 2. a college dance. 3. something added to spirits, such as soda or ginger ale.

mixologist, *n.* a bartender, a cir-cumlocutory term sometimes used for comic effect. (An American bartender, unlike most in England, spends much of his time mixing cocktails.)

mob, *n.* usually, a criminal gang.

mobile home, *n.* a house on wheels, often much larger than a caravan. It is built so that it can be moved from one site to another, but is not intended to be in continuous motion.

mobster, *n.* a member of a gang.

mocking bird, *n.* a native Ameri-can bird of the thrush family, that mimics other birds' sounds.

Model T, *n.* a machine or system that works reliably but lacks luxury appurtenances or sophis-tication. The term comes from the Model T Ford, the first-ever family car ("You can have it any colour providing it's black" —Henry Ford), which occupies a special place in the American folk memory.

molasses, *n.* dark treacle.

Mollybolt, *n.* a holder for a screw in a wall, similar to a Rawlplug. As with the latter, this is a brand name that has become common usage.

mom, *n.* mum.

monkey, *n.* used in combination,

someone who works at something with his hands; a grease monkey is a mechanic, a powder monkey in the navy is an explosives handler.

monkey wrench, *n.* an adjustable spanner.

moonlight, *v.* to do an extra job in addition to one's regular job.

moonshine, *n.* illegally distilled whisky. Also **moonshiner,** *n.* one who makes it.

mopboard, *n.* skirting board. Also called baseboard.

morning glory, *n.* an American plant of the *Convolvulaceae* family, with trumpet-shaped, brightly coloured flowers.

mosey, *n.* to stroll, go casually.

mossback, *n.* and *adj.* a person of antiquated conservative views.

mother, *n.* man, used in a pejorative sense. This is actually the first half of a term so obscene that it exceeds the bounds of native British speech.

motorman, *n.* the driver of a tube train or tram.

mountain oyster, *n.* the cooked testicles of a lamb or bull, reckoned a delicacy in some rural areas.

mourners' bench, *n.* at revivalist religious meetings, a bench at the front set aside for mourners or penitent sinners.

movie, *n.* motion picture. **movie theater,** *n.* cinema.

M.P., *n.* military policeman.

muff, *n.* vagina, Obscene.

muffler, *n.* silencer on a car.

mug shot, *n.* a photograph of a person taken for official purposes.

mugwump, *n.* a political independent or a group standing between the two main parties. It was current around the turn of the century, as a description borne proudly. But then a critic defined it as a bird that sits on the fence, with its mug on one side and its wump on the other.

mule skinner, *n.* mule driver.

muley saw, *n.* a saw with a long stiff blade, with motion directed by clamps at each end, mounted on guide rails.

mulligan stew, *n.* Irish stew.

mu-mu, *n.* a long, loose-fitting, Hawaiian-style dress.

muskeg, *n.* a bog formed in a depression of land.

muskrat, *n.* a native North American rodent, an aquatic animal with webbed feet and smooth, dark brown fur.

muss, *v.* to mess up, make untidy; e.g., the Air Force general in *Doctor Strangelove* on the prospects of success in a nuclear strike on Russia: "I don't say we wouldn't get our hair mussed, but we could get away with maybe 20 million dead."

mutt, *n.* (colloq.) a mongrel dog.

mutual fund, *n.* almost the same as a unit trust.

national guard, *n.* the military force of a state, composed of part-time soldiers, which becomes part of the national armed forces in time of war.

navy yard, *n.* naval dockyard.

neckerchief, *n.* a small scarf worn at the throat.

New Deal, *prop. n.* rhetorical term for the domestic policies of Franklin D. Roosevelt.

newsboy, *n.* a boy who sells or delivers newspapers.

newsman, *n.* journalist.

nickel, *n.* a five-cent coin.

nickelodeon, *n.* 1. an early cinema, usually with an entrance price of a nickel. 2. a jukebox.

nightclub, *n.* a night spot with drinks and entertainment; not a club in the sense that only members are admitted or even that there are any members.

night crawler, *n.* a worm used as bait in fishing. One British motorist driving through an American small town, seeing this advertised on a sign, assumed it was a quaint term for a motel with places for late travellers.

nightgown, *n.* nightdress.

nightstick, *n.* a policeman's truncheon.

nip-and-tuck, *adj.* neck-and-neck.

nipple, *n.* a nipple or a teat. (See **teat** in the British/American section.)

Nisei, *n.* first-generation Japanese-American.

nit-pick, *v.* to criticize on small details; a graphic metaphor much used.

nitty-gritty, *n.* (colloq.) the hard details.

normal school, *n.* teacher training college. They are rarely called this today, but many were some years ago.

nosh, *n.* used in its correct Yiddish sense, unlike in Britain, to mean a light snack between meals.

notions, *n.* haberdashery and other small items.

nudnik, *n.* (colloq.) a silly, dreary person, viewed with pity. Leo Rosten, in *The Joys of Yiddish,* says the education explosion in America has thrown up a new word, *phudnik,* which means a nudnik with a Ph.D.

nut pine, *n.* a native North American pine tree bearing edible nuts.

nuts, *n.* (colloq.) testicles.

oatmeal, *n.* porridge.

obfuscate, *v.* to confuse or cloud an issue.

observation car, *n.* a railway carriage, usually at the end of the train, designed to give the passengers a good view of the scenery.

ofay, *n.* a common Negro term for a white. It is pig Latin for foe, and this is popularly believed to be its derivation, but Dr. Dalby (see under **bug**) says it comes from Mandingo.

oilers, *n.* oilskins.

Old Faithful, *prop. n.* a geyser in

the Yellowstone National Park that erupts every 57 minutes exactly. Hence, anything or anyone totally reliable.

old fashioned, *n.* a popular and colourful cocktail, consisting of bourbon, bitters, sugar, and fruit. "An old-fashioned glass" is not a piece of antique tableware, but a small glass with a flat heavy base, and about the volume of a wineglass, in which an old fashioned is properly served.

Old Glory, *prop. n.* the American flag.

oleo, *n.* margarine. Short for oleomargarine.

olive drab, *n.* the cloth of which U.S. Army uniforms are made.

one-horse town, *n.* a very small town. The first known use of the term is in Mark Twain: "This poor little one-horse town"—from *The Undertaker's Chat.*

open primary, *n.* a primary election in which anyone can vote for any nominee regardless of party.

opine, *v.* to give an opinion.

orchestra, *n.* the front stalls in a theatre.

ordinance, *n.* bylaw.

outfit, *n.* a group of people working together, or a unit in the army.

outhouse, *n.* outdoor toilet.

outlet, *n.* electric power point.

outrider, *n.* a motorcyclist riding as escort.

overalls, *n.* a boiler suit.

overpass, *n.* flyover.

ox bow, *n.* a sharp bend in a river or the land enclosed in such a bend.

oyster cocktail, *n.* oysters served with trimmings.

Pacific Time, *n.* the Westernmost of the four time zones in the Continental United States.

pacifier, *n.* a baby's dummy.

paddle, *v.* to spank with a paddle.

paddle tennis, *n.* a hybrid of tennis and squash, played outside with paddles.

palisade, *n.* a stretch of steep cliffs. To New Yorkers, the Palisades is the long stretch of cliffs facing Manhattan across the Hudson River.

palooka, *n.* (colloq.) a guy or fellow. Usually inferior. The term originally meant a broken-down boxer.

panhandle, *n.* a narrow projecting strip of territory, as the Texas panhandle and the Laos panhandle.

panhandler, *n.* a beggar.

pants, *n.* trousers. Pants in the English sense are underpants or drawers (see Introduction).

pantyhose, *n.* tights. Tights refer to ballet tights.

paperhanger, *n.* decorator.

paraffin, *n.* paraffin wax. What in Britain is paraffin is kerosene in America.

parakeet, *n.* budgerigar, and related small parrots.

Parcheesi, *n.* a dice and board game, originating in India, but popular in many American homes.

parka, *n.* anorak. An Eskimo word.

Parker House roll, *n.* a kind of soft roll, first served at the Parker House hotel in Boston.

parking lot, *n.* car park.

parkway, *n.* a broad thoroughfare, usually landscaped with trees and plots of grass.

parlay, *n.* an accumulator bet.

parlay, *v.* (colloq.) to make money multiply.

parley, *n.* conference. This word is seen mostly in headlines.

parlor car, *n.* a luxurious railway carriage with individual armchair seats.

parochial school, *n.* church school, usually Roman Catholic.

party-pooper, *n.* (colloq.) someone who refuses to join in the fun.

pastrami, *n.* smoked beef, highly seasoned, popular as a sandwich filler.

patrolman, *n.* an ordinary policeman.

patrol wagon, *n.* black maria.

patsy, *n.* (colloq.) someone who is being manipulated by others.

pay dirt, *n.* soil which contains valuable minerals, as found by a prospector. Much used metaphorically; e.g., "Treasury investigators are striking pay dirt

in their drive against tax evasion."—Chicago *Daily News,* August 1, 1965.

pay station, *n.* a telephone call box.

pazazz, *n.* (colloq.) vigour, bounce.

pea jacket, *n.* a Navy-style duffel coat.

peasant, *n.* (colloq.) an ignorant yokel, or someone acting in a boorish, ill-mannered way.

pecan, *n.* an American nut, popular as a flavouring.

pecker, *n.* (colloq.) penis. The Englishman in North America should beware of using the phrase "Keep your pecker up."

peeler, *n.* (colloq.) strip dancer.

peg pants, *n.* tapered trousers.

pemmican, *n.* a concentrated mixture of lean meat and melted fat. An American Indian dish.

penny, *n.* a cent.

period, *n.* full stop.

persimmon, *n.* a native American fruit, orange-coloured and about the size of a plum.

pesky, *adj.* (colloq.) irritating, troublesome.

Phi Beta Kappa, *n.* an academic fraternity restricted to those who graduate from university with the highest academic honors. A Phi Beta Kappa key is the key-shaped badge, customarily worn on the watch chain.

Philadelphia lawyer, *n.* a lawyer who is particularly wily and cagey. Oddly enough, the term appears to have originated in England. According to Mitford

Mathews' *Americanisms*, the *Universal Asylum and Columbia Magazine* published in America in 1788 carried a letter from a correspondent in London saying that people there were using the expression "It would have puzzled a Philadelphia lawyer!" The correspondent could not think how it originated.

phonograph, *n.* record player.

pianola, *n.* an automatic piano. Originally a brand name.

piazza, *n.* this also means a porch.

picayune, *adj.* trifling, petty.

pick, *n.* pickax.

pickerel, *n.* any of the smaller kind of pike.

pick-up, *n.* pick-me-up.

pickup truck, *n.* an open lorry.

piker, *n.* a mean, stingy person.

pile driver, *n.* a huge, mechanically operated hammer, used in demolition work to pulverize masonry.

Pilgrim Fathers, *prop. n.* the English Puritan colonists who founded the first colony in New England at Plymouth, Massachusetts, in 1620.

pinch hit, *v.* in baseball, to substitute for the batter; hence to substitute for someone in any job or role. Also **pinch hitter.**

pinkie, *n.* little finger.

pinochle, *n.* a popular card game.

pint, *n.* 28.87 cubic inches liquid measure, or 33.6 cubic inches dry measure. There is only one British pint, 34.68 cubic inches.

pit, *n.* the part of an exchange devoted to special business, e.g., the grain pit.

pit, *v.* to remove the stones from fruit, such as cherries.

pitcher, *n.* 1. jug. 2. in baseball, the man who throws the ball to the batter. **pitcher's mound,** *n.* the slightly raised piece of ground on which the pitcher stands.

pitman, *n.* a connecting rod on a machine.

place, *n.* on the racecourse, coming in second, instead of second or third, as in Britain.

plank, *n.* a point on a political platform.

plastic wrap, *n.* a thick plastic wrapping used mostly for food.

plate, *n.* the anode of a radio valve.

play, *n.* a team's action in American football, hence, a strategic move toward a goal.

playbill, *n.* theatre program.

plebe, *n.* first-year cadet at a military academy.

pledge, *v.* on campus, to commit oneself to join a fraternity or sorority, or to be so committed.

plotz, *v.* (colloq.) collapse, fall down, fail catastrophically.

plug, *n.* a piece of tobacco.

plug ugly, *n.* thug.

plurality, *n.* more votes than any other contender, but not an absolute majority. An American would say that the Conservatives, because they got fewer votes than Labour and Liberals combined in 1970, won the election with a plurality.

pocketbook, *n.* handbag.

pocket veto, *n.* a Presidential veto of a Congressional bill in which the President simply ignores it instead of, as in another form of veto, sending it back with his objections. It can still become law by a further and more difficult process.

podiatrist, *n.* chiropodist. A new word that takes its place alongside the old.

Podunk, *prop. n.* originally an American Indian place name, it now stands for any small and insignificant place; e.g., overheard in a snack bar, "They gave the job to some jerk from Podunk U. because he's got a degree." First syllable pronounced to rhyme with "doe."

poison ivy, *n.* a leaf, indigenous to North America, which, when touched, causes a painful skin rash. Also **poison oak** and **poison sumac,** related leaves with similar effects.

pol, *n.* professional politician. Seen mostly in newsprint.

polecat, *n.* a skunk, or one of several related animals.

police, *v.* to clean and keep clean an outdoor area.

police dog, *n.* an Alsatian. Also called a German shepherd.

policy, *n.* a kind of lottery that used to be conducted illegally in poor city districts.

Pollyanna, *prop. n.* someone characterized by a sunny, everlasting optimism, named after the heroine of a popular sentimental novel of that name published in 1913.

pony, *n.* a crib, a paper from which exam answers are copied.

pony up, *v.* to pay a debt.

pooch, *n.* (colloq.) dog.

pool, *n.* a game played with 15 balls on a billiards table, often called a **pool table** in America.

poop, *n.* (colloq.) gen, information. A **poop sheet** is a document containing information.

pooped, *adj.* (colloq.) tired out, exhausted. (See also **party-pooper.**)

popsicle, *n.* an ice cream on a stick.

pork barrel, *n.* (colloq.) pertaining to gain from public office, either to enrich the officeholder corruptly, or to enrich his constituents as an inducement to reelect him.

porpoise, *n.* dolphin.

porterhouse, *n.* a cut of steak from the part next to the sirloin.

possum, *n.* the common word for an opossum, a marsupial animal indigenous to North America, resembling a larger rodent.

play possum, *v.* (colloq.) to pretend to be asleep or dead, as an opossum does.

post exchange, see **P.X.**

potato chips, *n.* potato crisps.

potlatch, *n.* a ceremony among some North American West Coast Indians at which the chief gives away things ceremonially, or else burns them, to show that he can afford to. Often used about conspicuous and wasteful consumption.

pot roast, *n.* a dish of meat braised in a casserole.

powdered sugar, *n.* icing sugar or confectioner's sugar.

prairie schooner, *n.* a romantic term for the covered waggons in which the pioneers travelled westward.

precinct, *n.* a district for election and police purposes.

predicate, *v.* to found or base a statement on something, e.g., "This is predicated on the fact that he's seen the plan and approves it."

prep school, *n.* a private secondary school and boarding school, with some social cachet, very approximately equivalent to a public school in Britain.

prickly pear, *n.* a pear-shaped cactus fruit. It is not unknown in Europe, apart from its familiarity to T. S. Eliot's readers. In Bernard Shaw's *Man and Superman,* when the brigand Mendoza captures Jack Tanner and his party in the Sierra Nevada, he offers them a meal of boiled rabbit and prickly pears.

primary election, *n.* an election in which voters in a state choose the candidate of a particular party from among several nominees. There are Democratic and Republican primaries in some states before the party conventions at which the two Presidential candidates are chosen.

prince, *n.* (colloq.) a fine man, praiseworthy fellow.

professor, *n.* a senior member of the teaching staff at a college or university, but not necessarily the head of a department. There may be several professors in one department, plus assistant professors. Hence, the status is not so elevated as it is in Britain.

prom, *n.* a dance, usually at a school or university. An abbreviation of "promenade."

prowl car, *n.* police patrol car.

psyched, *adj.* in tune with a situation, in a profoundly understanding way.

public school, *n.* a municipally-run school, the opposite of a private school. In many cities primary schools are called P.S.— followed by a number, the initials standing for "public school."

publisher, *n.* a newspaper proprietor. The word is used in this sense much more than in Britain.

pueblo, *n.* an Indian village in the Southwest, or a tribe of Indians who live there.

puke, *v.* to throw up.

Pulitzer prize, *prop. n.* one of several prizes awarded annually for excellence in the arts, letters, and journalism, named after the

Hungarian-born American Joseph Pulitzer.

pull-off, *n.* a lay-by on a motorway.

pumpkin, *n.* an indigenous North American squash, large, round, and dull orange in colour.

pumps, *n.* dancing shoes.

punchball, *n.* a kind of street baseball requiring no equipment but a rubber ball, which is punched rather than hit with a bat.

punk, *adj.* trashy, worthless. **punk,** *n.* a low, despicable person; tough-guy language.

Purple Heart, *n.* a medal awarded to any serviceman wounded in action.

purse, *n.* handbag. A purse (British) is a "change purse."

pushcart, *n.* barrow.

pussy, *n.* (colloq.) vagina. A lightweight, friendly word for it, even though obscene; it has none of the aggressiveness of other synonyms, and is never used as a term of abuse.

put down, *v.* to take down several pegs, to crush, metaphorically. As a noun, it becomes **put-down,** e.g., "That remark was a put-down."

P.X., *n.* post exchange, a shop in a military camp, roughly equivalent to a NAAFI.

quart, *n.* 57.8 cubic inches liquid measure, or 67.2 cubic inches dry. A British quart has 69.4 cubic inches.

quarter, *n.* twenty-five cents, a 25-cent coin.

quarterback, *n.* a key position in American football, the man who often carries the ball and decides the next move.

quarterback, *v.* to decide the next move or line to be followed, e.g., "It is even more true today than it was yesterday that people should not quarterback their own investments."—Paul A. Samuelson, financial columnist.

quarter section, *n.* a tract of land one-half-mile square.

quirt, *n.* a riding whip of braided leather.

quit, *v.* to leave, go away; to desist from some action, e.g., "I'll quit talking about this." To pack up, stop working, as in "The engine has quit." **quits,** *adj.* even, with all debts discharged. "Now we're quits" means that there is nothing owed on either side. Like a number of American words, these were in common use in England three and four centuries ago.

quitter, *n.* someone who gives up easily, who leaves the regiment under fire. "This is no time for quitters or talk of instant surrender."—Secretary of State William Rogers on Vietnam.

Quonset hut, *n.* a Nissen-type hut.

rack, *n.* (colloq.) bed, as in "I'm going to hit the rack." A variation of "sack" common among young folks.

raft, *n.* a large quantity, shoals, as "a raft of letters was received."

railroad, *n.* railway.

raincheck, *n.* a promise of the same thing at another time instead. When you buy a ticket to an outdoor sporting event in the Northern states, you can also buy, at a small extra cost, a raincheck. This entitles you to another ticket free if the event is postponed because of bad weather. This word is often adapted to other situations.

raise, *n.* a rise in salary. A "rise" to an American often means a male erection, so British talk of "getting a rise" can provoke an unexpected response.

raisin bread, *n.* currant bread.

rambunctious, *adj.* riled, uncontrollable, in temperament or mood.

rampike, *n.* a broken or dead tree that still stands.

ranch house or **ranch-type house,** *n.* a long, single-storey house with open-plan interior, common in new suburbs.

rap, *n.* (colloq.) talk, chat. This is a modern word, introduced by black Americans through the hip argot.

rare, *adj.* underdone, of meat.

rathskeller, *n.* a place, usually below ground, for festive drinking. A German word.

raunchy, *adj.* crudely sexy.

real estate, *n.* property.

realtor, *n.* estate agent. The word was invented in 1915 to give the profession more style, by the Minneapolis Real Estate Board, according to H. L. Mencken.

ream, *v.* (colloq.) to treat someone badly, give a raw deal. Since it also means, to a workman, to widen a hole (there is a tool called a "reamer") its derivation is clear.

Reconstruction, *n.* the period following the American Civil War in the defeated South. An "unreconstructed Southerner" is one with pre–Civil War attitudes.

receiptor, *n.* in law, a person who holds attached property until litigation ends.

recess, *n.* a break between classes at school or any other such break.

redcap, *n.* a railroad porter, so called because they traditionally wear red caps with their uniform. A vanishing breed.

redneck, *n.* (colloq.) a yokel, usually Southern.

red-eye gravy, *n.* a gravy made by adding water to the grease from cooked ham.

redwood, *n.* the wood of the Sequoia tree, much used in furniture. Some of the giant redwood trees in northern California are the oldest trees, and, in fact, the oldest living things, in the world.

reform school, *n.* an approved

school, an institution for juvenile lawbreakers.

regent, *n.* a member of the governing board of a college or university.

regular, *adj.* this also means normal, ordinary; "regular coffee" is coffee with cream and sugar; a "regular guy" is a square, allround, normal fellow.

relief, *n.* supplementary benefits; welfare payments to someone who is destitute.

remittance man, *n.* someone who lives on checks sent from home, or remittances. "There was that breed of English younger sons who became known throughout the West as remittance men." From *Tales of the Old Timers* by Frederick Bechdolt.

rent, *v.* hire. One rents furniture, a car, a flat, etc.

reserve bank, *n.* one of the twelve banks attached to the Federal Reserve Bank, the National Bank.

rest room, *n.* ladies' or men's room.

résumé, *n.* curriculum vitae.

revenue officer, *n.* an official who enforces the laws against illegal production of liquor. A figure in many folk songs.

rib roast, *n.* a joint taken from the forequarter.

riffle, *v.* 1. to leaf through papers. 2. to shuffle a pack of cards.

ringer, *n.* (colloq.) 1. someone who looks like someone else. 2. in sport, an illicit substitute, such as a professional playing on an amateur team.

rip off, *v.* (colloq.) to steal. It's a hippie term, and is generally used approvingly.

rip-off, *n.* (colloq.) something that does not give value for money, that cheats the customer or the public. "The [television] show is another Channel 7 rip-off." *Village Voice,* the hip New York weekly.

rock, *n.* 1. a stone. 2. (colloq.) jewel.

rock and rye, *n.* rye whisky flavoured with a blend of fruits.

rockfish, *n.* striped bass.

rock-ribbed, *adj.* (colloq.) inflexible.

roll, *v.* to rob someone who is drunk or otherwise helpless.

romaine lettuce, *n.* cos lettuce.

rookie, *n.* a new recruit to a calling, used extensively about soldiers, sportsmen, and policemen.

roomer, *n.* a lodger. **rooming house,** *n.* a house in which rooms are let.

roommate, *n.* someone sharing a room, flat, or house.

root, *v.* to cheer on, as at a sporting event.

> Root, root, root for the home team,
> If they don't win it's a shame.
> —from the traditional song "Take Me Out to the Ball Game."

root beer, *n.* a kind of soft drink, popular with children.

Roquefort dressing, *n.* a salad

dressing flavoured with Roquefort cheese.

roughhouse, *n.* a fight, serious or in fun.

roundhouse, *n.* a wild, hard punch.

roustabout, *n.* an unskilled labourer.

rout, *v.* to get someone out of bed.

route, *n.* a delivery round, as newspaper route, mail route. Often pronounced "rout." (But curiously, if the word "route" is used as in Britain, it is pronounced as in Britain.)

rowboat, *n.* rowing boat.

R rating, *n.* a category of film (R stands for "restricted") similar to an AA in Britain; unaccompanied juveniles are not admitted.

rubber, *n.* a condom. If you ask for a rubber in a stationer's shop, you will be directed to a drugstore. You should ask for an "eraser."

rubber band, *n.* elastic band.

rubbers, *n.* rubber overshoes.

rubberneck, *v.* (colloq.) to go sightseeing, looking this way and that way.

rubbing alcohol, *n.* surgical spirits.

rube, *n.* a country bumpkin (short for Reuben, a common country name) .

ruby, *adj.* the 3½-point type known in Britain as brilliant.

rum, *n.* this often stands for all spirits, as in phrases like "the demon rum" and "rum-runners of the Prohibition era."

rumble, *n.* a street fight, especially between gangs.

rumble seat, *n.* dicky seat.

rummage sale, *n.* jumble sale.

rumpus room, *n.* recreation room.

run, *n.* a ladder in tights or stockings.

run, *v.* to stand for political office.

rush, *v.* on campus, to look for candidates for a fraternity or sorority. At universities where these operate, there is often a "rush week" when **pledges** (see) are recruited.

rush, *n.* a state of high exhilaration. The word comes from the drug culture, though it does not necessarily refer to drugs.

rutabaga, *n.* a yellow turnip.

rye, *n.* whisky made from rye, the commonest kind in the United States.

rye bread or **rye,** *n.* much lighter than most rye bread in England and often made without caraway seeds. Order a sandwich in America and you will be asked, "White or rye?"

sack, *n.* (colloq.) bed. A masculine word, used typically among the military or on campus.

sacroiliac, *n.* the base of the spine.

saddle shoes, *n.* leather shoes of two colours.

sad sack, *n.* a blunderer, a loser. Originally an army term.

safe deposit, *n.* a safe place to keep valuables. **safe deposit box,** n. strong box.

sailboat, *n.* sailing boat.

on sale, *adj.* at reduced price.

sales clerk, *n.* shop assistant. Pronounced "clurk."

sales tax, *n.* a tax, usually imposed by the local authority, that is added as a percentage to the purchase price of an article and passed on directly to the customer.

saloon, *n.* tavern.

sandbag, *n.* a bag filled with sand used as a weapon.

sandbag, *v.* (colloq.) to knock someone down with a blow on the head, as with a sandbag, or to floor him, metaphorically speaking.

sandbox, *n.* sandpit.

sandlot, *n.* a piece of waste ground in a city where kids play; "sandlot baseball" is a common term.

sanitary napkin, *n.* sanitary towel.

Saranwrap, *prop. n.* a polyethylene wrapping used mostly for food. Though this is a brand name, it tends to be used for many products of this type.

Saratoga trunk, *n.* a large travelling trunk with a rounded top. The term and the object are dated, as is the social position of the resort from which it draws its name, Saratoga Springs, New York.

sarsaparilla, *n.* a soft drink with this flavour.

sashay, *v.* (colloq.) to ambulate, to walk with some style and to some effect.

sass, *v.* to speak impudently or mockingly. Used with a personal object, e.g., "In those days rebellion was sassing the cop on the beat."

sassafras, *n.* a native American tree with aromatic bark and root. These are sometimes used for flavouring or to make a mild tea.

sawbuck, *n.* 1. (colloq.) a 10-dollar bill. 2. a wooden structure that holds something while it is being sawed.

scallion, *n.* a spring onion.

scalper, *n.* (colloq.) a ticket agent who charges an exorbitant commission.

schlemiel, *n.* (colloq.) a fool or sucker, but seen in terms of endearment. A Yiddish word.

schmaltz, *n.* literally, chicken fat, but it also means anything overladen with sentiment.

schmuck, *n.* someone who is stupid and, usually, nasty.

schnook, *n.* (colloq.) a sucker, fool. It comes from Yiddish, and like most Yiddish words for a fool, it is affectionate and pitying. Pronounced to rhyme with "book."

schooner, *n.* a large beer glass, hence, larger than a British schooner.

schnozzle or **schnozz,** *n.* (colloq.) nose.

score, *v.* 1. to attack verbally, criticize sharply. Used mostly in newsprint. 2. (colloq.) to make out with a girl. 3. (colloq.) to succeed in buying some marijuana, in the youth argot.

Scotch, *n.* what Americans call Scotch whisky. The word "whisky" includes rye and bourbon. An American will specify which he wants when ordering.

scow, *n.* a barge for carrying rubbish out to sea.

scratch, *v.* to remove from a list of contenders or candidates.

scratch pad. *n.* note pad.

scrod, *n.* a young Atlantic cod or haddock.

scuba, *n.* underwater swimming equipment. An acronym of "self-contained underwater breathing apparatus."

scuffs, *n.* loose-fitting informal shoes.

scuttlebutt, *n.* (colloq.) rumour, gossip. Originally a navy term.

seaboard, *n.* coastline. With reference to the United States one speaks, for some reason, of "the Eastern Seaboard," but the "West Coast," never of the "Western Seaboard."

Secret Service, *n.* a branch of the Treasury Department that investigates Treasury offences and also has the task of guarding the President and his family. The term does not refer to the C.I.A.

sedan, *n.* saloon car.

selectman, *n.* in some small towns, an elected member of the town government.

seltzer or **seltzer water,** *n.* soda water. From the German.

semester, *n.* a term at school.

seminary, *n.* a college for training clergymen of any denomination, not only Roman Catholic, as in Britain.

senior, *n.* a final-year student at high school or university.

senior citizen, *n.* retired person. A euphemism for "old man" or "old woman" introduced into the language by the press in recent years.

set, *v.* (a table) —lay a table.

set-up, *n.* water, soda, or some other soft drink for mixing with spirits, e.g., "You bring your own liquor and they make a small charge for set-ups."

sexist, *adj.* prejudiced against one sex, usually women, in the way that a "racist" is prejudiced against one race.

shack up, *v.* (colloq.) to live with someone of the opposite sex out of wedlock.

shad, *n.* a North American deep-bodied herring, a popular food.

shade, *n.* a window blind or awning.

shades, *n.* (colloq.) sunglasses.

shaft, *v.* (colloq.) to treat someone unfairly, usually with deceit.

shag, *v.* to run after, retrieve, or follow. A schoolboy baseball player: "I practiced shagging fly balls." A detective giving evidence: "I shagged the suspect right across town."

shakedown, *v.* to extort money.

shakedown cruise, *n.* a sea voyage to try out a newly-commissioned navy ship.

sharecropper, *n.* a tenant farmer who takes as his wage a part of the crop he farms.

shaver, *n.* (colloq.) a very small boy, a toddler.

shavetail, *n.* second lieutenant.

shay, *n.* a light, horse-drawn carriage. The word is a corruption of the French *chaise.*

shebang, *n.* (colloq.) 1. the lot, as in phrases like "the whole shebang." 2. a party.

sheeny or **sheenie,** *n.* (colloq.) Jew; a racist term, street argot, rather passé.

shellac, *n.* a high-gloss varnish.

shellacking, *n.* a resounding defeat, a drubbing.

shim, *n.* a thin strip of metal or wood, used in building.

shine, *n.* 1. a liking, e.g., "She took a shine to him right away." 2. (colloq.) a Negro.

shingle, *n.* a small sign advertising services.

shinny, *v.* to climb vertically a pole or tree by the hands and shins.

shirtwaist, *n.* woman's blouse, an old-fashioned term.

shoo-in, *n.* an easy victory in an election, a walk-over.

shoot, *v.* 1. send, a racy word, e.g., "I had a girl friend once, she belonged to this Book-of-the-Month Club. Soon as she'd finished one book, why, they'd shoot her along another." From *Picnic* by William Inge. 2. to play certain games. One shoots pool, or craps.

shoot!, *interj.* a common exclamation, rather rural and small-townish, clearly a euphemism.

shopping bag, *n.* carrier bag.

short ribs, *n.* a cut from the brisket of beef.

shorts, *n.* underpants, as well as short trousers.

shot, *n.* a measure of spirits.

show, *v.* to come in third in a horse race. An each-way bet in America is a bet on a horse to win, place, or show.

shower, *n.* a party to give presents to a prospective bride, often of a particular kind, like a "linen shower" or "china shower."

Shriner, *prop. n.* a member of the Order of Nobles of the Mystic Shrine, a Masonic-type brotherhood.

shrink, *n.* (colloq.) psychiatrist. Short for "head-shrinker."

shuck, *v.* to take off the outer shell or peel.

shyster, *n.* a shifty, dishonest person.

sick, *adj.* ill. This word applies to any kind of illness, not only nausea, as in Britain.

sideburns, *n.* sideboards.

sidekick, *n.* constant companion.

sidewalk, *n.* pavement.

sidewheeler, *n.* paddle steamer.

siding, *n.* a covering on the outside wall of a house.

silence cloth, *n.* the soft material that is sometimes put under a tablecloth. Also **silencer.**

silk-stocking, *adj.* wealthy, luxurious. The term goes back a long way ("I trust the Gores will find their levees crowded with silk-stocking gentry."—Thomas Jefferson, writing in his diary, in 1812), and the advent of nylon has not put it out of circulation.

Simon Legree, *prop. n.* a harsh taskmaster. Simon Legree was the cruel plantation boss in *Uncle Tom's Cabin.*

sinker, *n.* (colloq.) a doughnut (American-style), so called because it is often dunked in coffee.

skillet, *n.* a frying pan.

skin-flick, *n.* a film that exploits crudely nudity and sex.

skinny-dip, *n.* nude bathing.

sky pilot, *n.* (colloq.) a service chaplain.

slate, *n.* a list of proposed candidates for office.

sleeper, *n.* a person, event, or issue that appears unimportant but turns out to play a key role, e.g., "Busing is the sleeper in the 1972 elections."—*Newsweek,* June 10, 1972.

slingshot, *n.* catapult.

slowpoke, *n.* slowcoach.

slug, *n.* a counterfeit coin, such as might be put into a slot machine.

slumgullion, *n.* a meat stew.

slush, *n.* a crushed-ice drink.

slush fund, *n.* a fund set aside for secret payments.

smacker, *n.* (colloq.) dollar, used only in the plural. One might say "a hundred smackers," but never "a smacker."

smart, *adj.* clever. In school, at least, a term of approval.

smidgen, *n.* a small amount.

smoke-filled room, *n.* a back room at a political gathering where deals are hatched in private. The term came into use during the Republican Party convention of 1920, in a description of the process by which Warren G. Harding was nominated; it is credited to Kirke Simpson, an Associated Press reporter. It has now found its way into the dictionaries.

smokestack, *n.* chimney or funnel.

smudge, *n.* a smoky fire, usually lit to drive away insects, or give a signal.

snake fence, *n.* a zigzag fence made of horizontal rails coming together at an angle.

snatch, *n.* (colloq.) vagina. Mildly obscene. When I was broadcasting from Northern Ireland for an American radio service, I spoke once about British Army snatch squads on the streets at night, which provoked some merriment at the other end. The term is used less than it was in my campus days.

sneakers, *n.* gym shoes.

snow, *v.* (colloq.) to talk deceptively but soothingly. "What a technique that guy has. He'd start snowing his date in this very quiet, sincere voice—like as if he wasn't only a very handsome guy but a nice, sincere guy, too."—*The Catcher in the Rye,* by J. D. Salinger. **snow job,** *n.* (colloq.) a cover-up, a whitewash story.

soap opera, *n.* a daytime radio or TV series of domestic drama, designed to wring the emotions of a housewife audience, so called because the archetypes of the genre advertise soap.

socialite, *n.* someone who is distinguished for his or her social life and nothing else.

social register, *n.* a book detailing who's who in the social élite.

social security, *n.* old-age pension, or the system of paying for and receiving old-age pensions.

sock hop, *n.* an informal dance, typically an undergraduate event, at which people take off their shoes to dance.

soda or **soda pop,** *n.* any carbonated soft drink. Distinguished from soda water by the use of an article, e.g., "Let's have a soda."

soda cracker, *n.* a plain biscuit usually eaten with butter.

soda jerk, see **jerk.**

softball, *n.* a game similar to baseball, but played with a larger, softer ball and ten to a side instead of nine. It is played mostly by youngsters; there is no professional softball.

solicitor, *n.* a legal officer of a city or a town.

solitaire, *n.* the game of patience.

Solon, *n.* a legislator. The word comes from the name of the great lawmaker of ancient Athens. Seen only in newsprint.

sophomore, *n.* a student in the second year of his or her four-year course in secondary school or university. The word is itself a comment on that stage of life, in that it comes from the Greek words *sophos,* wise, and *moros,* foolish.

sorehead, *n.* a disgruntled or unjustly complaining person; a poor loser.

sorghum, *n.* a canelike grass with a sweet-tasting juice, or a kind of dark treacle made from the juice, traditionally Southern.

sorority, *n.* on campus, the female equivalent of fraternity (see **fraternity**) .

soul, *n.* an aspect of the black American spirit, involving direct access to basic emotions, free expression, and racial pride. Much used in combination, as **soul brother, soul food,** and **soul music.**

southpaw, *n.* someone who is left-handed. Originally a baseball term.

speakeasy, *n.* an illegal drinking place during the Prohibition years.

special delivery, *adj.* express, a postal term.

specialty, *n.* and *adj.* speciality.

speedway, *n.* motorway.

spic, *n.* (colloq.) a Latin or Latin-American. A racist term.

spiel, *n.* a story, speech, or harangue. **spieler,** *n.* someone who calls out the attractions to a crowd at a circus or other show.

spigot, *n.* a small tap on a barrel or a tank. In Britain, this means only the winding part of the tap.

spike, *v.* (colloq.) to add liquor to a nonalcoholic drink. In high schools, there is traditionally an attempt by students to spike the lemonade punch at the school dance.

spike heels, *n.* stiletto heels.

spitball, *n.* 1. a pellet made of chewed paper, as thrown by schoolboys. 2. in baseball, a ball with spit rubbed into one side which supposedly can make it curve in flight.

spook, *n.* (colloq.) 1. C.I.A. man. 2. Negro; a racist term.

spool, *n.* reel of cotton, wire, tape, etc.

square knot, *n.* reef knot.

squash, *n.* a genus of fruits, eaten as vegetables, that includes the marrow. The word is seen on American menus.

stag, *adj.* (colloq.) without a girl partner at a social event; "going stag" to a dance means going without a girl. "Chutzpah is going stag to a wife-swapping party."—contemporary joke.

stand-upper, *n.* a piece spoken directly into a television camera, what in British TV is called an "on-camera."

Stars and Bars, *n.* the flag of the **Confederacy** (see) .

state, *n.* and *adj.* one of the fifty states, or pertaining to state, as opposed to federal, authority. In a political context, it sometimes means the opposite of what it would mean in Britain. For instance, a campaign for more state control of education would be a campaign *against* centralization.

statehouse, *n.* the building which houses a state legislature.

stateside, *n.* back home in America.

state's evidence, *n.* evidence for the prosecution in a criminal case.

state trooper, *n.* state policeman.

state university, *n.* the university which every state has and supports, tuition being almost free to qualified residents of that state.

station wagon, *n.* estate car.

statutory rape, *n.* sexual intercourse with a girl below the age of consent.

steamer, *n.* double-boiler.

steer, *n.* a castrated bull or ox. **bum steer,** *n.* (colloq.) a bad tip, bad advice.

stenographer, *n.* shorthand-typist.

stickpin, *n.* tiepin.

stir, *n.* (colloq.) jail.

stockade, *n.* military prison.

stock company, *n.* repertory company. **summer stock** is a repertory company that works only in the summer holiday season, as many do.

stockyard, *n.* cattle yard.

stogey or **stogie,** *n.* (colloq.) a cheap cigar. First syllable pronounced to rhyme with "toe," the second given a hard *g.*

stomp, *n.* a stamping dance done to jazz music.

stomp, *v.* (colloq.) to stamp on someone when he's on the ground.

stool pigeon, *n.* (colloq.) an informer or spy in the ranks.

stoop, *n.* a stone porch separated from the street by several stone steps, seen on terraced houses in many American cities. The word comes from the Dutch *stoep,* and originated in New York when it was the Dutch colony of New Amsterdam.

store, *n.* shop. "Here's the grocery store and here's Mr. Morgan's drugstore. Most everybody in town manages to look into those two stores once a day."— from *Our Town* by Thornton Wilder. **store clerk,** *n.* shop assistant.

storm cellar, *n.* a cellar with an entrance outside the house where refuge can be taken during fierce storms.

storm door, *n.* a second door to a building for extra protection from storms. Also **storm window.**

stovepipe hat, *n.* top hat.

straight, *adj.* of a drink, neat, e.g., "straight whisky."

strawberry blonde, *n.* a girl with reddish-blonde hair.

strawberry shortcake, *n.* a shortcake topped with strawberries and whipped cream.

straw boss, *n.* a subordinate boss; chargehand.

straw poll, *n.* an informal poll of opinion.

streetcar, *n.* tram, as in *A Streetcar Named Desire.* The word "tram" is unknown in America.

streetlamp, *n.* lamppost.

strict constructionist, *n.* someone who interprets the American Constitution narrowly. Members of the Supreme Court and other national jurists are often divided into strict and loose constructionists.

strike, *n.* a baseball term. A batter is out when he has three strikes against him. The term is adapted to many situations; the meaning of "He had two strikes against him from the start," for instance, is clear.

stringer, *n.* a timber spanning a railway trestle or bridge.

stroller, an infant's pushchair.

struck jury, *n.* a jury chosen by agreement between two opposing lawyers in a court case, each striking out members of the group empanelled until the agreed twelve remain.

stump, *v.* to go on a political campaign, e.g., "He stumped New

England for Nixon." **stump orator,** *n.* rabble-rouser.

submarine sandwich, *n.* another word for **hero sandwich,** a section of French loaf with a lot of filling.

subway, *n.* tube train, or underground.

succotash, *n.* a mixture of corn and lima beans; a popular vegetable dish, it is indigenous, and the word also, which comes from a similar Iroquois Indian word.

sucker, *n.* lollipop. An *all-day sucker* is a huge one.

summation, *n.* a lawyer's closing speech in a court case.

summer soldier, *n.* someone who supports a cause only when the going is easy. The phrase is Thomas Paine's; in the darkest days of the American War of Independence, when many were deserting the cause, he wrote scornfully of "the summer soldier and the sunshine patriot," in *The American Crisis* pamphlets.

sunny-side up, *adj.* used about fried eggs, this means fried on one side only so that the liquid yoke beams upward.

superhighway, *n.* motorway.

surrey, *n.* a light, four-wheeled, horse-drawn carriage.

suspenders, *n.* braces.

sweat, *n.* (colloq.) trouble, effort, used mostly in the negative phrase "No sweat," meaning "It's no trouble."

sweatshirt, *n.* a soft, light pullover, especially as worn by athletes to prevent chill.

sweet potato, *n.* 1. a vegetable similar to the yam, and only distantly related to the potato, eaten widely instead of potatoes in the United States. It is indigenous to America as, indeed, was the potato originally. Among sweet-potato-eating people, ordinary potatoes are called white potatoes. 2. an ocarina, a musical instrument.

swing shift, *n.* an evening shift at work.

syndicate, *n.* a highly organized crime ring.

tab, *n.* bill.

table, *v.* to set aside a motion rather than discuss it. This is the exact opposite of the meaning in Britain. (See **table** in the British/American section.)

table cream, *n.* single cream.

tack or **thumbtack,** *n.* drawing pin.

tacky, *adj.* shabby, somewhat on the seedy side. The word has a small-townish flavour, e.g., the oft-quoted verdict of the Kansas City *Star* (December 2, 1931): "Englishwomen have the knack of looking tacky even when they are wealthy and titled."

tad, *n.* (colloq.) small boy. Short for tadpole.

taffy, *n.* toffee.

tailgate, *n.* the tailboard of a van or lorry.

tailgate, *v.* to drive very closely behind another vehicle.

take down, *v.* to take up a loan, i.e., to draw the money.

tamale, *n.* a Mexican dish popular in America, made of crushed corn, meat, and red pepper.

Tammany Hall, *prop. n.* the headquarters of the political machine that ran New York City politics for a long time, often used to signify boss-ruled or corrupt municipal politics.

tan, *v.* (colloq.) to smack, as in "I'll tan his hide."

tape, *n.* in television, videotape. In British TV studios, one would say "v-t."

tardy, *adj.* late. Used much in schools.

tart, *n.* tartlet.

taxi dancer, *n.* a girl who works in a dance hall and dances with customers for a price for each dance.

tea cart, *n.* tea trolley.

teamster, *n.* a vehicle driver. The term dates back to the days when he drove a team of horses, and now it is used almost only in the collective, about the "teamsters" as a labor force.

teed off, *adj.* angry, fed up.

teeny-bopper, *n.* a pre-teen-age pop fan.

teeter-totter, *n.* a seesaw.

teletypewriter, *n.* teleprinter.

temple, *n.* a synagogue other than an orthodox one.

tenderloin, *n.* 1. a filet steak. 2. the tenderloin district is the nightclub and brothel section of a town.

> Some write back home to the old
> folks for coin,
> That's their ace in the hole.
> And some got a gal in the ol'
> tenderloin,
> That's their ace in the hole.
> —Traditional jazz song

termite, *n.* a wood-eating white ant.

territory, *n.* an area under U.S. Government jurisdiction, with a certain amount of self-government, which does not have statehood. Puerto Rico and the Virgin Islands are territories; most states were territories before they were admitted to the Union.

terry cloth, *n.* a pile fabric, like bath toweling.

Thanksgiving, *n.* a national holiday, the fourth Thursday in November, traditionally a time of family reunions and fireside celebrations. It marks the end of harvesting the first crop by the Pilgrim settlers who landed in Massachusetts in 1620. A ritual Thanksgiving dinner includes turkey and pumpkin pie.

theme, *n.* in school or university, a composition.

Thirteen Colonies, *prop. n.* the original colonies which rebelled against British rule and became the United States.

Thousand Island dressing, *n.* mayonnaise with chopped pimentos and gherkins added.

thread, *n.* cotton.

threads, *n.* (colloq.) clothes. Used mostly by young people.

through, *adv.* 1. on the telephone, this means finished, not connected. If you tell an American telephone operator that you're through, she's likely to cut you off. 2. in time, until the end, e.g., "through July" means until July 31st.

throughway, *n.* a motorway with few access points or exits.

ticket, *n.* a list of candidates put forward by a party.

tic tac toe, *n.* noughts and crosses.

tights, *n.* ballet tights or similar. What in Britain are called tights are "hose" or "pantyhose."

timberline, *n.* the line in a mountainous or cold region beyond which trees do not grow.

tinhorn, *n.* (colloq.) a loudmouthed boaster making fraudulent claims, often used about gamblers.

Tom Collins, *n.* a long iced drink of gin, lemon juice, soda, and sugar, popular in the summertime.

ton, *n.* 2,000 pounds, a "short ton" in Britain.

tongue depressor, *n.* a doctor's spatula.

toque, *n.* a small hat with no brim.

torch singer, *n.* a female singer, who sings popular songs in a romantic, moody, usually sad vein.

tortilla, *n.* a thin pancake made from cornmeal. A Mexican dish popular in America.

Tory, *prop. n.* historically, one who remained loyal to Britain during the American War of Independence.

tote, *v.* to carry a heavy burden, as in "tote dat barge, lift dat bale . . ."—from the song "Ol' Man River."

touchdown, *n.* the scoring play in American football.

touch football, *n.* a mock-football (American), played by any number of people, in which a touch is substituted for tackle.

town meeting, *n.* a meeting of all the citizens of a village or small town, or else the qualified voters, to discuss and decide community issues.

track, *n.* 1. athletics, as in *track team* and *track meeting.* 2. racecourse.

track home, *n.* one of a row of houses in a street that are all the same.

tracklayer, *n.* a platelayer on the railway.

track record, *n.* past performance.

trade-off, *n.* an exchange of one concession or gain for another. Commonly used in modern discussion of international or business strategy.

traffic circle, *n.* roundabout.

trailer, *n.* caravan.

tramp, *n.* (colloq.) a near prostitute, a scrubber. A very insulting term. It has come into use since that song of the early 1940s, "The Lady Is a Tramp"; then it simply meant that the lady was gaily unconventional.

transom, *n.* fanlight.

trash, *n.* rubbish. **trash can,** *n.* dustbin.

trash, *v.* (colloq.) to wreck, vandalize; a word from the hippie argot.

trick or treat, *n.* the traditional children's cry to a householder on Halloween, meaning that unless they are given a present, usually sweets, they will carry out some destructive prank.

trimming, *n.* defeat.

trolley, *n.* tram.

truck, *n.* 1. a lorry, or waggon. **fire truck,** *n.* fire engine. 2. vegetables raised for the market. 3. a kind of dragging, distracted walk, a word from the drug culture.

trucker, *n.* 1. market gardener. 2. lorry driver.

trunk, *n.* the boot of a car.

tube, *n.* valve, as on a television or radio set.

tuckered or **tuckered-out,** *adj.* tired out, exhausted.

turkey, *n.* a loser. In the theater, it means specifically a flop.

turnpike, *n.* a road with tollgates.

turtleneck, *n.* polo neck.

tuxedo, *n.* dinner jacket, from the once-fashionable Tuxedo Park country club in New York.

twister, *n.* tornado.

two-fers, *n.* theatre tickets sold two for the price of one, when a theatre has plenty of empty seats.

ukase, *n.* an order from above. A Russian word that has come into the American political vocabulary.

uncle, *n.* a token of surrender. In kids' fights, the demand "Say uncle!" means "Give up!"

Underground Railroad, *n.* before the American Civil War, a chain of people who helped runaway slaves, passing them along from one hiding place to another until they reached the Canadian border and safety.

undershirt, *n.* vest. A "vest" in America is a waistcoat.

unit rule, *n.* a rule whereby, at a political convention, a majority of delegates of one state cast the entire vote for that delegation. It was because California Democrats accepted the unit rule, after a bitter wrangle, that Senator George McGovern won the Democratic nomination on the first ballot at the 1972 convention.

upgrade, *adj.* uphill; **on the upgrade** means improving, getting better.

upset price, *n.* reserve price, as at an auction.

uptight, *adj.* tense and intense; often means very conformist.

uptown, *n.* and *adj.* away from

the centre of the city and toward the more residential areas; or, as a direction, the opposite of **downtown** (see).

vacuum bottle or **vacuum flask,** *n.* Thermos flask.

valedictorian, *n.* the student who delivers the so-called valedictory oration at the graduation ceremony. This is an honour.

vamoose, *v.* (colloq.) scram. It comes from the Spanish.

Vandyke, *n.* a pointed beard. Groucho Marx once, off-screen: "I can't remember; did Ulysses S. Grant have a Vandyke or did Vandyke have a Ulysses S. Grant?"

vaudeville, *n.* music hall.

veep, *n.* (colloq.) the Vice President of the United States, a contraction of V.P.

venire, *n.* a panel from which a jury is chosen.

vest, *n.* waistcoat.

vest pocket, *adj.* designed to fit into a waistcoat pocket, hence, miniature.

veteran, *n.* an ex-serviceman of any age.

Veterans Day, *prop. n.* Armistice Day.

Victrola, *n.* record player. The original trade name when the instrument was invented, it is somewhat dated now, but still used.

visiting fireman, *n.* a visitor from out of town, particularly someone come to see the big city.

Volstead Act, *prop. n.* the amendment to the Constitution forbidding the sale of alcoholic beverage, which brought in Prohibition. **Volstead Era,** the Prohibition years.

WAC, *n.* Women's Army Corps.

WAF, *n.* Women in the Air Force, equivalent of the WAAF.

Waldorf salad, *n.* a salad made up principally of diced apples, celery, nuts, and mayonnaise.

walking papers, *n.* (colloq.) the sack from a job, or forced departure of any kind. If a girl breaks off a romance, it may be said that "She gave him his walking papers."

walk-up, *n.* a room or flat on an upper storey in a building that has no lift.

walleye, *n.* pike perch.

Wall Street, *prop. n.* the New York financial world; the term is the equivalent of "the City." It is actually the main street in the financial district of New York.

wampum, *n.* Indian bead money. A childish colloquialism for "money."

warden, *n.* the governor of a prison.

ward heeler, *n.* a minor official of a political party who performs small duties on a local, i.e., ward, level.

washcloth, *n.* flannel.

wash up, *v.* to wash oneself, not the dishes. Philip French recalled in a *New Statesman* article that he once suggested to his American hostess that he help her wash up, and was met with a startled look.

WASP, *n.* an acronym for White Anglo-Saxon Protestant, the dominant ethnic group in the United States.

Wassermann test, *n.* the standard test for syphilis. In some states, it is compulsory before marriage.

water cooler, *n.* a machine that holds and dispenses cold drinking water, usually along with paper cups. Most offices in America have one.

water tower, *n.* a tower, raised above the ground, that serves as a reservoir for small towns.

WAVES, *n.* women serving in the United States Navy. The letters stand for "women accepted for volunteer emergency service."

wax paper, *n.* greaseproof paper.

way, *adj.* very or very far, as in "It's way over that way." **way back,** *n.* a long time ago.

West Point, *prop. n.* the location of the U.S. Military Academy, and the common name for the Academy; equivalent of Sandhurst.

wetback, *n.* (colloq.) an illegal immigrant. The term comes from the Southwest, where Mexicans used to swim across the Rio Grande to enter the United States illegally.

whipping cream, *n.* double cream.

whippoorwill, *n.* a nocturnal bird with an insistent call. Until a few years ago, it was a feature of the Southern states, but has now migrated in large numbers to New England.

whistle-stop, *v.* to travel about the country by train on a political campaign.

whistle-stop town, *n.* a small, unimportant town, so called because the train stops there only when signaled by a whistle.

white-haired boy, *n.* (colloq.) blue-eyed boy, favourite. Also called **fair-haired boy.**

white lightning, *n.* crude, fierce, homemade whisky. As Marge says in *The Landlord* (the novel and the film), "It's ruthless, just ruthless!"

whole wheat, *n.* wholemeal.

whomping, *adj.* enormous, usually in a metaphorical sense rather than as physical description, e.g., "a whomping increase of $150 a week."

wienie or **wiener,** *n.* a sausage, like a cocktail sausage. **wienie roast,** *n.* a party at which sausages are roasted, a common teenage social event.

wild, *adj.* (colloq.) in addition to its literal meaning, this means far-out, fantastic. Two examples heard in conversation: a traveller returned from the Far East: "We got into some wild situa-

127

tions." Someone talking about a girl: "She's got a wild build!"

wildcat strike, *n.* unofficial strike.

windbreaker, *n.* windcheater.

window shade, *n.* blind or awning.

windshield, *n.* windscreen.

Windy City, *prop. n.* Chicago.

wing, *n.* fender on a car.

wing dam, *n.* a barrier to protect a riverbank from erosion by a fast current.

wingding, *n.* (colloq.) big party or "bash."

wino, *n.* an alcoholic down-and-out.

wire, *n.* telegram.

wire service, *n.* a news agency that distributes its news by teleprinter, like Reuter and the Associated Press.

Wobbly, *n.* (colloq.) a member of the I.W.W., the Industrial Workers of the World, a radical movement in the early years of this century, whose most famous martyr was Joe Hill.

wood alcohol, *n.* methylated spirits.

wood trim, *n.* woodwork in a house.

wop, *n.* (colloq.) an insulting term for an Italian-American.

workout, *n.* bout of strenuous exercise.

work over, *v.* (colloq.) to beat up systematically.

World Series, *prop. n.* the climax of the baseball season, at the end of the summer, a series of up to seven games between the champions of the two leagues.

wrangler, *n.* a cowboy who breaks in wild horses.

wrap, *n.* a woman's coat or other outer garment.

write-in, *v.* to vote for a candidate whose name is not on the ballot paper by writing it on. Also used as a noun.

Y, *n.* the Y.M.C.A. or Y.W.C.A., or usually the hostel that these organizations run in most big cities. Used in phrases like "staying at the Y."

yak or **yakkety-yak,** *v.* and *n.* (colloq.) talk, chatter.

yam, *n.* a sweet potato (see) and some related tuberous vegetables.

Yankee, *prop. n.* among most Americans, a native of one of the New England states. Among Southerns, any Northerner. An Englishman I met once was travelling back through the United States from Mexico, and was entertained by some people in Tennessee. Talking about business in Mexico, he remarked that there was a lot of Yankee money and enterprise down there. There was a cool silence after this, and then someone said resentfully, "Well, I'll bet there's some rebel money and rebel enterprise down there too."

yard, *n.* any area around a home, whether it is carpeted with concrete, grass, or flowers. Most British front or back gardens would be called "yards" in America. The word "garden" is usually used only if it is cultivated with special, almost professional, care, or is used for growing vegetables.

yardbird, *n.* convict.

yegg, *n.* a petty thief. A dated and rather literate colloquialism.

you-all, *pron.* "you" in the South. Its use is popularly taken as the mark of a Southerner. Non-Southerners doing an imitation always use this in addressing an individual, but most Southerners insist that it is used only in addressing a group of people. As H. L. Mencken remarks in a dissertation on this word, the subject is fraught with bitterness.

zap, *v.* (colloq.) hit, knock down, kill.

zee, *n.* zed, the last letter of the alphabet.

zero, *n.* nought.

zip code, *n.* postal code.

zip gun, *n.* a homemade gun that fires a projectile by means of a spring.

zonked, *adj.* (colloq.) 1. stoned, high on drugs. 2. struck, knocked out, usually metaphorically.

zucchini, *n.* courgette. Pronounced "zookeenee."

Useful Lists of Some British Words in This Dictionary

Accommodation

bed-sitting room
block of flats
detached house
fixtures and fittings
flat
freehold

housing estate
maisonette
semi-detached
service flat
terraced house

Household

airing cupboard
carrier bag
chesterfield
conversion heater
cotton wool
drawing pin
earth wire
eiderdown
french polish
garden
geyser
greengrocer
gripewater
hob

ironmongery
loo
lumber room
methylated spirits
morning room
muslin
nappy
paraffin
primus stove
Rawlplug
scullery
serviette
trolley
yard

Food

Banbury cake	kipper
Bath bun	marrow
biscuit	minced meat
broad bean	mixed grill
bubble-and-squeak	pasty
bun	pease pudding
butty	plaice
castor sugar	porridge
char	rissole
chicory	rock cake
chipolata	rock salmon
chips	runner bean
cockle	saveloy
coley	savoury
corn flour	Scotch egg
corned beef	shepherds pie
cos lettuce	silverside
crisps	single cream
crumpet	skate
currant bread	sprat
digestive biscuit	squash
double cream	Stilton
doughnut	swiss roll
flan	tart
gammon	toad-in-the-hole
gateau	treacle
hake	whelk
joint	wholemeal
kedgeree	

Drink

bitter	light ale
brown ale	nip
Burton	pale ale
dram	plonk
egg flip	scrumpy
lager	shandy

small beer	whisky
stingo	whisky mac
stout	

School and Campus

A-levels	O-levels
Cantabrian	Oxbridge
college	Oxonian
comprehensive school	plough
county school	polytechnic
dormitory	prefect
eleven-plus	prep
fag	prep school
first	primary school
G.C.E.	professor
grammar school	redbrick
headmaster, head	rusticate
instructor	secondary modern school
long vac	send down
mistress	Wykehamist

On the Road

accumulator	junction
big end	lay-by
bonnet	level crossing
caravan	lorry
central reservation	L-plate
charabanc	motorway
coach	nearside
dual carriageway	number plate
estate car	offside
gear lever	petrol
hood	tailboard

Clothes

anorak	braces
boiler suit	dinner jacket

132

draper
dressing gown
hacking jacket
jumper
knickers
mackintosh
nightdress
oilskins
pants

pinafore
plimsolls
stiletto heels
suspenders
tights
trousers
turn-ups
vest
windcheater

Business and Finance

Consols
current account
deposit account
director
gazump
gearing
gilt-edged
hire purchase
limited company

managing director
never-never
purchase tax
shares
stag
stocks
supertax
unit trust
V.A.T.

Politics

alderman
back benches
caucus
Chancellor of the Duchy of Lancaster
Chancellor of the Exchequer
Chequers
Conservative
Labour Party
Liberal Party
Lord Chancellor
Lord Privy Seal
Lords

mayor
Privy Council
provost
Statute of Westminster
table
Tory
Treasury Bench
U.D.I.
Unionist
Westminster
Whitehall
woolsack

Useful Lists of Some American Words in This Dictionary

Accommodation

American plan
apartment
condominium
duplex
efficiency

European plan
frame house
housing project
piazza
ranch house

Household

ashcan
bureau
cheesecloth
cladding
clapboard
closet
coaster
color wash
cot
cotton
cupboard
davenport
drapes
faucet
garbage
heater

highboy
kerosene
kettle
lowboy
Mollybolt
paraffin
plastic wrap
Saranwrap
shellac
shopping bag
sink
skillet
spool
tea cart
wax paper

Food

angel food cake
apple butter
baloney
beet
betty
biscuit
blueberry
bluepoint
Boston cream pie
brownie
buckwheat
catsup
cherrystone clam
chicken à la king
chiffon
chuck steak
coffee cake
cookie
corn bread
corn dodger
corned beef
corn pone
cornstarch
crab apple
devil's food cake
dill pickle
doughnut
eggplant
English muffin
fig newton
finnan haddie
French fried
French toast
grits
ground meat
ground round
gumbo
half-and-half

hamburger
hard sauce
hero sandwich
hominy grits
huckleberry
hush puppy
iceberg lettuce
Jell-O
jelly roll
lima bean
liverwurst
maple sugar
meat loaf
molasses
mountain oyster
mulligan stew
oatmeal
oleo
oyster cocktail
Parker House roll
pecan
pemmican
persimmon
porterhouse
pot roast
powdered sugar
pumpkin
red-eye gravy
rib roast
rockfish
romaine lettuce
Roquefort dressing
scallion
short ribs
soda cracker
squash
succotash
sweet potato

table cream
tamale
tart
tenderloin
Thousand Island dressing

tortilla
Waldorf salad
whipping cream
zucchini

Drink

applejack
bock beer
bourbon
chaser
eggnog
highball
hooch
Manhattan
martini

mint julep
mixer
old fashioned
rock and rye
rye
Scotch
Tom Collins
white lightning

School and Campus

alma mater
alumnus
assignment
college
commencement
fraternity
freshman
grade school
grind
gut course
high school
honor system
junior

junior college
normal school
parochial school
Phi Beta Kappa
prep school
public school
recess
regent
senior
sophomore
sorority
state university
theme

On the Road

auto
back-up lights

clunker
coupe

crosswalk
divided highway
expressway
filling station
freeway
gearshift
hot rod
license plate
metallic road
mini-bike
muffler
parking lot

parkway
pickup truck
pull-off
sedan
station wagon
throughway
traffic circle
trailer
trolley
trunk
turnpike
windshield

Clothes

bathrobe
beanie
boat shoes
cut-offs
deck shoes
drawers
haberdasher
jumper
kicks
knickers
mu-mu
nightgown
pants

pantyhose
pea jacket
pumps
rubbers
shorts
suspenders
sweatshirt
terry cloth
tights
tuxedo
undershirt
vest

Business and Finance

blue-chip
bonds
bucket shop
building and loan association
certified check
chattel mortgage
checking account
commercial paper

common stock
Dow Jones
Dun & Bradstreet
fair trade
installment plan
leverage
mutual fund
reserve bank

Politics

administration	mugwump
alderman	New Deal
assembly	open primary
caucus	plurality
congressman	pocket veto
G.O.P.	pork barrel
Know-Nothings	selectman
liberal	smoke-filled room
manifest destiny	table
mayor	unit rule

73 74 75 76 77 10 9 8 7 6 5 4 3 2 1